Twayne's English Authors Series

EDITOR OF THIS VOLUME

Sylvia F. Bowman

Indiana University

William Caxton

TEAS 263

After that I had accomplysshed and fynysshed dyvers
hystoryes as wel of contemplacyon as of other hysto-
ryal and worldly actes of grete conquerours & pryn-
ces / And also certeyn bookes of ensaumples and doctryne /
Many noble and dyvers gentylmen of thys royame of Englond camen and demaunded me many and oftymes / wherfore
that I have not do made & enprynte the noble hystorye of the
saynt greal / and of the moost renomed crysten kyng / Fyrst
and chyef of the thre best crysten and worthy / kyng Arthur /
whyche ought moost to be remembred emonge us englysshe
men tofore al other crysten kynges / For it is notoyrly knowen
thorough the unyuersal world / that there been ix worthy & the
best that euer were / That is to wete thre paynyms / thre Jewes
and thre crysten men / As for the paynyms they were tofore the
Incarnacyon of Cryst / whiche were named / the fyrst Hector
of Troye / of whome thystorye is comen bothe in balade and in
prose / The second Alysaunder the grete / & the thyrd Julyus
Cezar Emperour of Rome of whome thystoryes ben wel kno-
and hadd / And as for the thre Jewes whyche also were tofore
thyncarnacyon of our lord / of whome the fyrst was Duc Jo-
sue whyche brought the chyldren of Israhel in to the londe of
byheste / The second Dauyd kyng of Jherusalem / & the thyrd
Judas Machabeus of these thre the byble reherceth al theyr noble hystoryes & actes / And sythe the sayd Incarnacyon haue
ben thre noble crysten men stalled and admytted thorough the
unyuersal world in to the nombre of the ix best & worthy / of
whome was fyrst the noble Arthur / whos noble actes I purpose to wryte in thys present booke here folowyng / The second
was Charlemayn or Charles the grete / of whome thystorye is
had in many places bothe in frensshe and englysshe / and the
thyrd and last was Godefray of boloyn / of whos actes & lyf
I made a booke unto thexcellent prynce and kyng of noble me-
morye kyng Edward the fourth / the sayd noble Jentylmen
Instantly requyred me tenprynte thystorye of the sayd noble
kyng and conquerour kyng Arthur / and of his knyghtes
wyth thystorye of the saynt greal / and of the deth and endyng
of the sayd Arthur / Affermyng that I ought rather tenprynte
his actes and noble feates / than of godefroye of boloyne / or
ij

A page of Caxton's Prologue to his
editon of *Le Morte d'Arthur*

83-11

WILLIAM CAXTON

By FRIEDA ELAINE PENNINGER

University of Richmond

TWAYNE PUBLISHERS
A Division of G. K. Hall & Co.
Boston, Massachusetts, U. S. A.

Published in 1979 by Twayne Publishers,
A Division of G. K. Hall & Co.
All Rights Reserved

Printed on permanent/durable acid-free paper and bound
in the United States of America

First Printing

Library of Congress Cataloging in Publication Data

Penninger, Frieda Elaine.
William Caxton.

(Twayne's English authors series; TEAS 263)
Bibliography: p. 150-165.
Includes index.
1. Caxton, William, ca. 1422-1491—Criticism and interpretation.
2. England—Intellectual life—Medieval period, 1066-1485.
PR1848.P4   828'.2'09   78-31585
ISBN 0-8057-6759-2

for my mother
Lena Young Penninger

Contents

About the Author

Frieda Elaine Penninger, professor of English at the University of Richmond, Virginia, holds the Bachelor of Arts degree from the Woman's College of the University of North Carolina and the Master of Arts and Doctor of Philosophy degrees from Duke University. She is a member of Phi Beta Kappa, the Modern Language Association of America, the Southeastern Renaissance Society, the Medieval Academy of America, and the Southeastern Medieval Association. She is listed in *The Directory of American Scholars* and in *Contemporary Authors*.

Professor Penninger has edited *A Festschrift for Professor Marguerite Roberts* and has compiled an annotated bibliography, *English Drama to 1660 (Excluding Shakespeare)*, for the Gale Research Company Information Guide Series. Her *William Caxton* explores the fifteenth century world view which emerges from the books published by Caxton and studies Caxton's contribution to English letters as publisher, editor, translator, and essayist.

Preface

William Caxton's claim to a place in English literature rests on five principal grounds. First, as the founder of the earliest English printing press, he published some one hundred and eight items over a period of twenty years. The long endurance and the large output of his press constitute one of Caxton's contributions. Second, a substantial number of the titles Caxton chose are popular or semipopular accounts in the fields of science, history, philosophy, religion, and sociopolitical theory and practice. These books provided his peers with access to contemporary thought; they provide us with access to the general world view of the late fifteenth century. Third, Caxton translated twenty-six of the books he published and two which he did not publish; he was, therefore, responsible for the prose style of a substantial number of the printed books available in English to his peers. Fourth, eleven of his translations that are in the form of prose narratives were precursors to the genre of the novel; he published a body of important English poets: Geoffrey Chaucer, John Gower, and John Lydgate; he thus made English belles-lettres available in print. Fifth, Caxton's own prologues and epilogues to thirty-three of his published books make him one of the notable English essayists.

Caxton has often been studied as a printer; to a lesser degree, he has been examined in the context of the political world of his day; but the present study places emphasis on late fifteenth century thought as it is reflected in Caxton's books and on his contributions to literature. Caxton's own interest was in the books which he issued from his press, not in the mechanics of its operation. The evidence that this statement is true rests in Caxton's prologues and epilogues, in which he says very little about the functioning of the press but a great deal about the books he has read, translated, and edited. He mentions kings, princes, prelates, noble lords and ladies, citizens, and children, but always in the same connection: their relationship to the books he is printing. The books Caxton published bear another kind of witness to his values: They are durable and readable, but they are not elegant; he does not appear on the usual lists of "fine printers"; he did not invent new processes for printing or quickly acquire advanced techniques. He was concerned with using the press to put words into enduring and accessible form, not with creating elegant examples of the typographer's art. The focus of his interest and of ours is, then, the nature and content of his books.

FRIEDA ELAINE PENNINGER

University of Richmond
October 16, 1978

Acknowledgments

As the notes and bibliography indicate, I am heavily indebted to many scholars for what their research has discovered about William Caxton. I should also like to acknowledge most gratefully help from a number of other sources. During the summers of 1965 and 1967, as a fellow of the Southeastern Institute of Medieval and Renaissance Studies, and frequently since, I have made use of the libraries of Duke University and of the University of North Carolina at Chapel Hill. The institute, a part of the Duke–University of North Carolina Co-operative Program in the Humanities and initiated with a grant from the Ford Foundation, makes the extensive holdings of the libraries of these universities available to scholars in an atmosphere conducive to thought and work. The University of North Carolina's Hanes Foundation for the Study of the Origin and Development of the Book proved highly useful. The fellows of the institute, particularly Senior Fellow R. M. Lumiansky, listened to and advised me.

Two of the Duke University reference librarians, Miss Mary Whitfield Canada and Miss Florence Blakely, rendered indefatigable and intelligent aid. Dr. Curt F. Bühler, Miss Louise C. Houllier, and Dr. Paul Needham of the Pierpont Morgan Library answered various inquiries and made available microfilms of the Morgan's copies of *The Book of Divers Ghostly Matters*, *Infantia salvatoris*, *Le Morte d'Arthur*, *Moral Proverbs*, and a Sarum *Horae*. I am grateful to the Pierpont Morgan Library, its director, Dr. C. A. Ryskamp, and its trustees for permission to reproduce a photograph of a page of Caxton's Prologue to his edition of *Le Morte d'Arthur*, Pierpont Morgan Library Accession number 17560, as the frontispiece of this volume. Examining incunabula in the Morgan and in the British Museum enhanced the pleasure of my work. The Library of Congress has come to my aid. The staff of the Boatwright Memorial Library of the University of Richmond and particularly Mr. Ardie L. Kelly, formerly its head librarian, and Miss Kathleen Francis, have rendered extensive assistance.

I should like to thank the council of the Early English Text Society for permission to quote from various of its editions of Caxton's books.

Quotations from Caxton's prologues and epilogues are essentially from the Early English Text Society edition by W. J. Blyth Crotch. Other quotations from Caxton's texts and from *The Winchester Malory* are from the society's editions, from microfilm issued by University Microfilms, Ann Arbor, Michigan, or from the Morgan Library copies mentioned above. For the greater ease of the modern reader, the Middle English quotations, except in a few special instances, have been given modern English spelling, punctuation, paragraphing, and capitalization, though I have kept Caxton's word order and vocabulary as nearly as possible.

I should like to record my appreciation to Professor Jean R. Buchert of the University of North Carolina at Greensboro and to Professor Marianne R.B. Duty of John Tyler Community College, who read parts of the manuscript, and to Dr. Mary Beaty of Davidson College and Professor Georgia B. Christopher of the University of Richmond, who read it all. Professor Robert H. Wilson, of the University of Texas, has graciously answered several inquiries. I should like to thank the University of Richmond for a grant from the George J. and Effie L. Seay Educational Fund. Finally, I should like to thank my mother, who has ungrudgingly spent her time to free mine.

Chronology

This chronology lists the first editions of the books in which any significant free composition by William Caxton occurs but excludes simple translations. Unless later editions are shown individually, they repeat with only minor variants the matter of the first one. Key books without original matter by Caxton also appear. The order follows George D. Painter's; the dates of publication are from Painter, E. Gordon Duff, N. F. Blake in *Caxton and his World*, and *The New Cambridge Bibliography of English Literature*, where dates are inferential.

[1415/1424]   William Caxton's birth in Kent, possibly in 1422.

[1438]   Apprenticeship fee paid for Caxton by Robert Large, London.

1463   First records of Caxton as governor of the English nation, Bruges.

1469–1470   Last records of Caxton as governor.

1471–1472   Caxton's residence in Cologne, where he learned to print.

[1475], [1473—1474]   Caxton's translation of Raoul Lefèvre's *The Recuyell of the Historyes of Troye*, the first book printed in English, published by Caxton in Bruges.

[1475], [1476]   Caxton's translation of Jacobus de Cessolis, *The Game and Play of the Chess*, first edition, printed by Caxton in Bruges.

[1476]   Probable date of the indulgence, issued during the papacy of Sixtus IV, which may be the first piece of printing done by Caxton at Westminster.

[1477], [1479]   Caxton's edition of his own translation of Raoul Lefèvre's *Jason*.

1477   First dated book, *The Dicts or Sayings of the Philosophers*, first edition, printed by Caxton at Westminster; translated by Anthony Woodville, Earl Rivers, from the French compilation by Guillaume de Tignonville.

1478   Christine de Pisan, *The Moral Proverbs*, translated by Anthony Woodville, Earl Rivers.

[1478]   Geoffrey Chaucer, *The Canterbury Tales*, first edition anywhere of a printed text, without prologue or epilogue. *Boethius de consolatione philosophiae*, translated by Geoffrey Chaucer.

1479   *The Cordial*, translated by Anthony Woodville, Earl Rivers, from the French version by Jean Mielot.

[1479], [1477]   Caxton's *Advertisement*.

[1480]   *Vocabulary in French and English*, probably translated by Caxton from the anonymous French-Flemish *Livre des mestiers de Bruges*.

1480   Anonymous, *Chronicles of England*, first edition. *Description of Britain*, extracted by Caxton from Ranulf Higden's *Polychronicon*, which had been translated from Latin into English by John Trevisa. Caxton's translation of *The Metamorphoses of Ovid*, not known to have been printed by Caxton.

[1481]   *The Mirror of the World*, first edition, translated by Caxton from the French prose *Image du monde* by Gossouin (Gautier?) de Metz. *Reynard the Fox*, first edition, translated by Caxton from the Dutch *Hystorie van Reynaert die Vos* (anonymous).

1481   Cicero, *Of Old Age;* Cicero, *Of Friendship;* and Bonaccursius de Montemagno, *The Declamation of Noblesse; Of Old Age* possibly in Caxton's translation. *Godfrey of Boloyne* (also called *The Seige of Jerusalem* or *Eracles*), translated by Caxton from *Estoire de Eracles empereur et la conqueste de la terre d'outremer*, a French translation based on William of Tyre's *Historia rerum in partibus transmarinis gestarum*.

[1482]   Ranulf Higden, *Polychronicon*, translated from Latin into English by John Trevisa and printed by Caxton, with an eighth book added by Caxton.

[1482], [1483]   *The Game and Play of the Chess*, second edition, with a new Prologue.

1483   John Lydgate, *The Pilgrimage of the Soul*.

14[8]3   John Gower, *Confessio amantis*.

[1483], [1484]   Alain Chartier, *The Curial*, translated by Caxton. Geoffrey Chaucer, *The Canterbury Tales*, second edition, with a Prologue. Geoffrey Chaucer, *The Book of Fame*. Anonymous, *The Life of Our Lady*, first edition.

[1483]   Pietro Carmeliano, *Sex epistolae*.

1484   Caxton's translation of *The Knight of the Tower*, from *Livre . . . pour l'enseignement de ses filles* by Geoffroy de la Tour Landry.

[1484], [1483]   Caxton's translation of *Caton*, attributed to "Dionysius Cato."

1484   Caxton's translation of *Fables of Aesop*.

[1484]   Anonymous, *The Order of Chivalry*, translated by Caxton.

[1484], [1483]   Jacobus de Varagine, *The Golden Legend*, first edition, translated by Caxton.

1485   Sir Thomas Malory, *Le Morte d'Arthur*. *The Life of Charles the Great*, translated by Caxton from *Fier a bras*, a French prose work attributed to Jean Dagnyon. Anonymous, *Paris and Vienne*, translated by Caxton.

[1487], [1486], [1484]   *The Royal Book*, translated by Caxton from Lorens d'Orleans, *Somme (Livre) des vices et des vertus*, or *Somme le roi*.

[1487? 1485?], [1485]   *The Life of Saint Winifred*, translated from the Latin (of Prior Robert?) by Caxton.

1487   Jacques Legrand, *The Book of Good Manners*, translated by Caxton.

[1488], [1489]   *Reynard the Fox*, second edition, with an Epilogue which is probably not Caxton's. *Four Sons of Aymon*, translated by Caxton from a prose version of a *chanson de geste*. Anonymous, *Blanchardin and Eglantine*, translated by Caxton.

1489, [1490]   Christine de Pisan, *Feats of Arms*, translated by Caxton.

[1489]   Anonymous, *Doctrinal of Sapience*, translated by Caxton.

[1490]   *Eneydos*, translated by Caxton from the anonymous *Livre des Eneydes*, of which Virgil's *Aeneid* is not the immediate source. Anonymous, *The Art and Craft to Know Well to Die*, translated by Caxton.

[1491]   *The Book of Divers Ghostly Matters* (a three part tract, Part One translated from Henricus Suso, *Horologium sapientiae;* Part Two, anonymous, *Twelve Profits of Tribulation;* Part Three, an abridged *Rule of St. Benedict*). *The Fifteen Oes*, attributed to St. Birgitta, translated by Caxton. Caxton's death.

CHAPTER 1

William Caxton

WILLIAM Caxton established the first printing press in England. As many as one hundred and eight editions, or eighty-seven different titles that are attributed to Caxton—works that range from an advertisement of seven lines to Ranulf Higden's *Polychronicon*, 900 pages, and Jacobus de Varagine's *Golden Legend*, 896 pages—survive.[1] Caxton himself translated twenty-six of the books he printed, he also translated *Vitas patrum*, although it was not published until after his death, and his Ovid's *Metamorphoses* was perhaps not printed until this century. He edited some of the books he printed so extensively as to make them in part his books. Through his work as printer, translator, and editor, Caxton to a substantial degree shaped the popular and general reading matter of England in the last quarter of the fifteenth century; and through his essays, written as prologues and epilogues for certain books he published, he became the critic and historian of the English incunabulum period. The books from his press range over the broad spectrum of the century's interests; they make possible the reconstruction of a fifteenth century world view. Caxton is, therefore, singularly significant as a medium for exploring fifteenth century English letters.

I   *Brief Historical Background*

In 1376, one hundred and one years before the first dated book appeared from Caxton's press in Westminster, Edward the Black Prince, heir apparent to the English throne, died.[2] When the Black Prince's father, Edward III, died in 1377, the Prince's ten year old son succeeded his grandfather as King Richard II. In 1399, John of Gaunt, Duke of Lancaster, son of Edward III and uncle of Richard II, died, leaving the enormous Lancaster estates to his son, Henry Bolingbroke. While Bolingbroke was in exile, Richard II confiscated the Lancaster property; but, when Bolingbroke returned to England, he recovered the Lancaster lands and also captured the crown as Henry IV.

Richard II died in prison—how has not been established with certainty. A section which Caxton added to his edition of Ranulf Higden's *Polychronicon*, which was printed in 1482, offers two versions of the deposed king's death. The first relates that when various nobles rose against Henry IV in support of Richard II, many of them were seized and executed. Then:

When King Henry saw that these lords thus had risen and assembled great people to have put him to death and for to restore King Richard again to his crown and to his realm, [Henry] thought to eschew [avoid] such perils. Anon [he] commanded Sir Piers of Exton that he should go straight to Pontefract [Castle] whereas King Richard was in prison, the which was set at table for to dine. And anon [soon] after, Sir Piers came into the chamber where the king was, and eight men with him and each man an axe in his hand. Truth it is when the king saw Sir Piers with his fellowship enter into the chamber defensibly [protectively] arrayed, he shoved the table from him and sprang in the midst of them & wrought an axe out of one of their hands, and set himself valiantly at defense. And himself defending, he slew four of the eight. And when the said Sir Piers saw the king so defend him, he was sore abashed and greatly afeared. And forthwith started upon the place whereas King Richard was wont to sit. And as King Richard fought and defended himself going backward, the said Sir Piers smote him on the head with his axe that he fell to ground. Then cried King Richard, "God mercy." And then he gave him yet another stroke on the head, and so he died.

And thus was this noble king slain and murdered. And when the king was dead, the knight that had thus slain him set him down by the dead body of King Richard. And [he] began to weep, saying, "Alas, what thing have we done? We have put to death him that hath been our king and sovereign lord two and twenty year. Now have I lost mine honor. Nor I shall never come in place but I shall be reproached. For I have done against mine honor."

The *Polychronicon* then reports another version of Richard's death, that he committed suicide by starving himself, and comments that, whichever version is true, "Certainly he died."[3] Modern historians can do no better than to repeat these accounts.

Henry IV's reign, begun on the battlefield, continued in strife. The Hundred Years' War with France, which had started in Edward III's time, dragged on. Discord in Scotland and Wales; rebellion among the nobles in England; and unrest in the church, including the long-continued political and theological controversy occasioned by the papal schism and also the impulse toward reformation indicated by the Lollard movement, marked his reign. Henry IV, who ruled from 1399 to his death in 1413, was succeeded by his son Henry; and Henry V, who reigned from 1413 to 1422, gave England a glorious if ephemeral victory at Agincourt and married the French princess, Catherine of Valois. When this "mirror of all Christian kings"[4] died, he left as heir to the English throne a son, also Henry, who was then only eight months old.

After Henry VI became king in 1422—the year when, it is generally supposed, Caxton was born—he ruled during the period of the chaotic Wars of the Roses, when the descendants of the houses of Lancaster and York vied for the crown. Since Henry VI apparently inherited a tendency to insanity through his mother's family, Henry V's marriage to Catherine of Valois, which might have helped to heal the troubles between England and France, created instead a new problem at home. Another French woman, Joan of Arc, turned the tide of the Hundred Years' War; but she was burned as a witch in 1431. Henry held the throne from 1422 to 1461, was deposed, returned to rule briefly in 1470–1471, and was murdered.

Edward IV, the son of Richard, Duke of York, who took the throne from Henry VI, reigned from 1461 to 1470 and from 1471 to 1483. After Edward IV made a secret and romantic marriage to Elizabeth Woodville, the widow of Sir John Grey, in 1464, Elizabeth bore him in 1470 his first son, Edward, heir apparent to the throne, and in 1472 his second son, Richard, Duke of York. Henry VI's queen, Margaret, fought for the rights of her own son Edward, but in 1471, Edward IV captured Margaret and, so the story runs, occasioned the death not only of her son, Prince Edward, but also of her husband, Henry VI.

Caxton's career was linked particularly to the reign of Edward IV and to Edward's sister Margaret, who married Charles, Duke of Burgundy. Caxton resided "by the space of .xxx. year for the most part in the countries of Brabant, Flanders, Holland, and Zeeland."[5] He knew Margaret personally; she became his patron and benefactor. He also knew Edward's brother-in-law, Anthony Woodville, Earl Rivers; Caxton printed three books translated by Rivers, *The Dicts or Sayings of the Philosophers* (1477, [1480], [1489]), *The Moral Proverbs* of Christine de Pisan (1478), and *The Cordial* (1479). As we examine Caxton's prologues and epilogues, we shall see the names of these and other members of the royal family weave themselves into the early history of English printed books.

Among the grim ironies of history is the fact that Edward IV's brother, Richard, Duke of Gloucester, in a move much like Edward's

own pursuit of power, seized the throne at Edward IV's death and
deposed the young Edward V, who reigned only from April to June of
1483 and who died, again according to the usual account,[6] in the
Tower of London at his uncle's direction. Earl Rivers was regent for
the young Edward V when the boy king and his brother were seized
and taken to the Tower. Richard of Gloucester, who caused Rivers to
be beheaded at Pontefract Castle on June 25, 1483, ruled briefly from
1483 to 1485 as Richard III. In 1485, the year when William Caxton
printed Sir Thomas Malory's *Le Morte d'Arthur*, Henry Tudor, Earl
of Richmond, defeated Richard III at the Battle of Bosworth Field
and ascended the throne as Henry VII, the first of England's Tudor
monarchs.

Although political and military turmoil touched the lives of English
citizens of all stations, the effect was often remote and indirect. The
daily experience of hundreds of English men, women, and children
told them, however, that life was "nasty, brutish, and short";[7]
poverty and disease were widespread and uncontrolled; ignorance
was rampant. If the fifteenth century has had an inconspicuous place
in English literary history, perhaps the reason lies in part with such
unsettled and unhappy times. The only literary date commonly
recalled between the death of Chaucer in 1400 and the accession of
Elizabeth I in 1558 is Caxton's publication of Malory's *Morte d'Arthur*
in 1485; and this identification of a century with a printer is no
accident. Caxton's books enable us to capture the quality of life in his
century with far more wholeness than do the stories of kings and
killings. Caxton's work demonstrates how life went on in those
difficult years; how values transcending crowns and battles held their
own; how the literary life of England was sustained, even in a century
when few great literary men were at work; and, perhaps most
importantly, how the human spirit held to the hope of finding
meaning, pattern, and even happiness.

II *Caxton's Early Career*

Documents concerned with Caxton's life are not extensive. Official
papers sometimes refer to him, as does a friend and fellow printer,
Wynkyn de Worde; but no record has survived of such simple facts as
the date of his birth or the name of his wife.[8] What survives, however, is Caxton's life preserved in his books. By examining what
Caxton translated, edited, and printed, and by examining what he

said about himself, his work, and his books, we can follow a Medieval mind revealed through Medieval materials and directed toward a Medieval end: the betterment of the human lot not only in time but also in eternity.

Caxton's comments about his life are preserved, as we have observed, in the prologues and epilogues he wrote for thirty-three of the books he printed. He says that he was born in the Weald, or wooded area, of Kent. Although the exact date of his birth is not recorded, the year 1422 has been deduced, since he was presumably apprenticed in 1438 at the age of sixteen. George D. Painter has challenged this date on the grounds that 1438 is not a firm date in itself, that the payment may not mark the beginning of his apprenticeship, and that the apprenticeship may not have begun at sixteen. Painter proposes the range 1420–1422.

The record of Caxton's education is bare. He remarks that the English spoken in his native Kent was "broad and rude" (Crotch, p. 4); he thanks his parents for having sent him to school. Since contemporary records show that he was apprenticed to Robert Large of London, a prosperous mercer or wool merchant who was also warden, sheriff, and lord mayor of London, Caxton's training for business occurred in the city of London and in the household of a wealthy and prominent man. A book Caxton later printed, *The Book of Courtesy* [1477–1478],[10] provides insight into the Medieval view of etiquette and education, for this work is directed to young boys who need instruction in manners, morals, and education generally. Eighteen of its seventy-six stanzas are devoted to the recommendation of poets:

> Exercise yourself also in reading
> Of books enornede [adorned] with eloquence;
> There shall ye find both pleasure & learning. . . .
>
> (Stanza 45)

The Book of Courtesy advises that the boy should know the great English poets—John Gower, Geoffrey Chaucer, Thomas Hoccleve, and John Lydgate:

> Lo, my child, these fathers ancient
> Reaped the fields fresh with fulsomeness.
> The flowers fresh they gathered up & held
> Of silver language, the great riches;

> Who will it have, my little child, doubtless
> Must of them beg; there is no more to say,
> For of our tongue they were both lock & key.
>
> (Stanza 58)

Although Caxton as printer made Gower, Lydgate, and especially Chaucer available, *The Book of Courtesy* contains a wealth of other, more practical advice: do not throw rocks at animals; do not repeat gossip; do not overeat; give special heed to the rich. It has spiritual advice as well, counseling prayers and attendance at divine service. Whether at home in Kent or in Large's house in London, Caxton must have been trained much in the manner described in *The Book of Courtesy*. He learned to move through the world of the powerful, assuming his place without presuming on it, as his own prologues indirectly testify.

When and how Caxton's apprentice years ended is not known. Perhaps as early as 1441, the year of Large's death, Caxton moved from London to Bruges. By 1463, he was governor of the English nation, or the head of the company of merchant adventurers—Englishmen who were engaged in trading, chiefly in wool, and who resided in the Low Countries. The wool trade was important, economically and diplomatically; and the governor of the English nation was charged with the general oversight of business.[11] As a result, Caxton came to know persons of consequence in England and in Burgundy, and several records of correspondence survive from his governorship. The details of his Bruges years are scant, for Caxton himself states merely that he lived for thirty years in Brabant, Flanders, Holland, and Zeeland but that he never journeyed into France.

Although Caxton left the post of governor of the English nation about 1470, the precise date of his departure, the reason for it, and what he did immediately thereafter are not shown in the records which survive. Speculation has suggest that restrictions governing the English nation caused Caxton to give up the governorship, perhaps to marry. (Only the record of the divorce of his daughter Elizabeth from Gerard Crop indicates that he had married.) George Painter has recently argued, however, that life as governor of the English nation was less confining than earlier studies suggested and that Caxton lost the governorship as "a direct consequence of the Lancastrian restoration, and without his wish or intention."[12] However that may be, the end of the governorship must have ended an era in Caxton's life, and have brought him, perhaps unexpectedly, into a new world—the world of the printed book.

III   *Caxton's Beginnings as Translator and Printer*

It has generally been assumed that after Caxton left the governorship, he was employed by Margaret, Duchess of Burgundy and the sister of Edward IV of England, in connection with her own trade in wool or in her library, perhaps, but exactly what service Caxton performed for Margaret has not been discovered. Since our concern is with Caxton's literary work, however, the importance for us of his association with Margaret is that the earliest information about Caxton's interest in writing attributes his sustained efforts as a translator to Margaret's influence.

In the prologue to the first book that he printed independently, his own translation of *The Recuyell of the Historyes of Troye* [Bruges, 1475], Caxton records that he began to translate *The Recuyell* from the French text prepared by Raoul Lefèvre for Philip, Duke of Burgundy, but that he found the chore burdensome. He later showed several quires of his translation to Margaret, and with her corrections and at her "dreadful commandment," he completed the work in the hope of a continuation of her "yearly fee" and various "good and great benefits" to him. Caxton spells out the exact dates of his work on *The Recuyell* translation: "Which said translation and work was begun in Bruges in the Country of Flanders the first day of March the year of the Incarnation of our said Lord God a thousand four hundred sixty and eight. And ended and finished in the holy city of Cologne the .xix. day of September the year of our said Lord God a thousand four hundred sixty and eleven etc." (Crotch, pp. 5, 2).

What the "etc." at the end of this statement could conceivably mean is a question. A more interesting question, however, is what Caxton was doing in Cologne. Wynkyn de Worde, long Caxton's associate in his Westminster printing business, says that Caxton learned printing in Cologne, but it was not until 1923, when Colonel J. G. Birch rediscovered and publicized the records which indicate Caxton's residence in Cologne from mid-1471 to late 1472, perhaps as late as December, that de Worde came to be generally credited with knowing whereof he spoke.

Whether Caxton learned to print because he went to Cologne or whether he went to Cologne because he wanted to learn to print is an unsettled point. In 1470, when the temporary reseating of the deposed King Henry VI made life dangerous for a competing monarch, Edward IV left England and visited his sister Margaret in Burgundy. It is sometimes supposed that Caxton himself went to Cologne for reasons connected with the troubles of the English throne, but the facts now available do not allow for the resolution of this question.[13]

Although Caxton does not tell us where or how he learned to print, he does tell us why. In the Epilogue to Book III of *The Recuyell of the Historyes of Troye*, he states that when he had translated *The Recuyell*, he was so pressed by demands for copies that he found his pen "worn, mine hand weary & not steadfast, mine eyes dimmed with overmuch looking on the white paper, and my courage [heart, disposition] not so prone and ready to labor as it hath been," for his age was increasing. He therefore "practiced & learned at my great charge and dispense" to print, and he remarks about the marvels of printing multiple copies speedily. He also urges his readers to note that this book "is not written with pen and ink as other books are" but that "all the books of this story"—that is, all the copies of it—"were begun in one day and also finished in one day . . ." (Crotch, pp. 7-8).

IV   The *Printing Process and the Early Printed Book*

Although Caxton had the good fortune to be born into the century when the printing of books became a practical reality,[14] he rather surprisingly has very little to say about either the invention of printing or its development. In fact, the book Caxton added to Ranulf Higden's *Polychronicon* devotes only forty words to the subject; indeed, the invention of printing and the taking of four great fish are treated as if they were matters of equal note. In Book 8, Chapter 28, folio CCCCxxiii, of the *Polychronicon*, Caxton records for the year 1453 that "This year were taken four great fishes between Ecrethe and London; that one was called mors marine, the second a sword fish, and the other twain were whales." On the same folio appears this entry: "Also about this time the craft of enprinting was first found in Magounce in Almayne, which craft is multiplied through the world in many places, & books been had great cheap and in great number by cause of the same craft."

Scholars have reconstructed the process of the invention in some more detail than Caxton and his peers provide. Modern students attack the problem by establishing a precise definition of what printing means and by examining the essential components of the process. A printed text is distinct from a manuscript text in that the manuscript, as the word itself implies, is handwritten; each letter is shaped successively on the page to make up the text. Generally speaking, in printing, a section of text is transferred as a single unit onto the printing surface. Seals and stamps provided an early method of duplication; and although the impression made by a seal or stamp is not what is usually understood as printing, the process may have given rise to the idea of developing a method for printing verbal texts. If a text is cut in mirror image into a block of wood, the block inked, and the text transferred to paper or some other surface, the process is a form of printing called *xylography*. A fair number of "block books," or books with both the verbal text and the pictures printed from blocks, survive from the fifteenth century, when European printing emerged.

But if printing is defined as printing with movable type—*typography*—then xylography is not true printing. "Movable type" means that the letters (or, especially in early printing, an occasional combination of two or more letters) and other necessary symbols, such as punctuation marks, are cast each as a separate piece of type; and these types are then moved about in various combinations to make the text of a printed page. That is, a set, or font, of types can be repeatedly recombined to produce various texts. The two forms, xylography and typography, appear simultaneously in books with the text set in movable type and with the illustrations done from woodcuts or with woodcut initials.

The priority of Oriental printing over Occidental seems established. Beyond that fact, at least three views of the relationship of Oriental to Occidental printing are possible: that Europeans learned from the Orient to print with movable type; that xylography was brought from the Orient and then developed into printing with movable type; or that European printing developed independently of, though later than, Oriental printing. Leaving the Orient altogether out of the matter, there is argument about whether xylography developed into typography. Resolution of this last problem depends largely on the dating of early woodcuts and block books, and the dates cannot be absolutely established; but the evidence favors the probability of the development of xylography and typography as separate, contemporaneous events. In sum, the prevailing view is that European printing was invented independently both of Oriental printing with movable types and of any process of printing by xylography.

Chauvinism has led several nations to put forward candidates for the role of the inventor of the European printing process. Defining "the invention of printing" as the invention of a method of casting individual metal types, most recent students of the matter consider the inventor to have been John Gutenberg, who worked chiefly in Mainz, Germany (Caxton's Magounce in Almayne), in the second quarter of the fifteenth century. As is the usual case with scientific and technological developments, once the breakthrough to the possibility was made, the knowledge of the process spread rapidly. But England moved slowly; eight countries are said to have preceded England in acquiring presses.

Although it is largely agreed that William Caxton was the first English printer and operated the first press in England, the claim for his primacy has been challenged. A book from a press at Oxford, *Expositio in symbolum apostolorum,* bears the printed date, given in Roman numerals, of 1468. If this date could be established as correct, the case for an English printer before Caxton would be made. However, the remaining books from the early Oxford press are dated 1479 and after, and these books appear to students of printing to be of a group with the 1468 one. Errors in dates are common; Caxton's edition of John Gower's *Confessio amantis,* for example, bears the date, again in Roman numerals, of 1493, two years after his death. The silence of Oxford records about any pre-Caxtonian press there and the absence of any other comparably early Oxford book have led bibliographers to redate *Expositio in symbolum apostolorum* to 1478 on the reasonable assumption that an *X* was accidentally omitted in the Roman numerals of the printed date.

The argument for the priority of an Oxford press has had at least one interesting development. A seventeenth century printer, Richard Atkyns, published an elaborate story of how Henry VI, urged on by the Archbishop of Canterbury, commissioned Caxton and a second man to go to Haarlem and secretly bring away a workman who could instruct Englishmen in printing, and of how this man, by name Corsellis, printed at Oxford. Atkyns's story has a monetary motive, as Conyers Middleton soon established: The title of Atkyns's essay is "The original and growth of Printing; collected out of History and the Records of this Kingdom; wherein is also demonstrated, that Printing appertaineth to the Prerogative Royal; and is a flower of the Crown of England."

Middleton persuasively argues that Atkyns concocted his tale in order to persuade Charles II that the granting of printing privileges was a royal prerogative which could be extended to him, Atkyns. That there was a printer in England before Caxton is unproved and unlikely, but that one was spirited away from Holland by Caxton himself is more than unlikely.[15] Caxton's being the first English printer to establish a printing house which issued a significant body of books over a period of years is more to the point than is the question of absolute priorities, but the claim that Caxton is England's proto-typographer seems firmly grounded.

Any book printed in the fifteenth century is set apart under the name *incunabulum* to recognize the distinctiveness of early printing. The earliest printed books may lack a title page, though not all incunabula do; and no book printed by Caxton has a title page. The colophon, generally defined as an inscription or a device used to identify the publisher, is now likely to appear on the title page or near the beginning of the book; but in early books, it was, as its etymology suggests, a "final touch" that appeared at the end of the text. In Caxton's books, the colophon may be a longish statement giving author, title, translator, place and date of translation, publisher, place and date of publication, and various observations that arise from these facts.

Caxton also identified some of his books by a woodcut device.[16] Since such a device is intended to identify the publisher, its design must be in some way significant; Caxton's is clearly marked with his initials, "W C." Between the initials are two intertwined symbols which are sometimes presumed to be superimposed numerals, 47 or 74, that recall a date (or perhaps two dates, 1447 *and* 1474) that was of some significance in Caxton's career. These symbols are also, perhaps more often, regarded as representing the stamp with which Caxton, mercer, stamped merchandise. Two additional parts of the design appear to be the letters "S" and "C" in Roman letters. If these parts are indeed letters, then they may stand for "Sancta Cologna," for Caxton says he completed the translation of *The Recuyell of the Historyes of Troye* in Holy Cologne. That he would have used Roman letters on his device but never a font of Roman type seems to some scholars unlikely—but, say others, if the language is Latin, *Sancta Cologna*, the Roman style of letter perhaps struck Caxton as appropriate. In rows at the top and bottom of the device are small lozenges marked with an "X" and with black spots between them. The lozenges have been interpreted as cakes and the spots as stones that yield a rebus for Caxton's name, *cakes-stone*. Whatever the significance of the individual parts of its design, the device is one of the best known marks of Caxton's publishing.

This device has, however, another use, one beyond identifying Caxton's books. As the woodblock used for printing the device progressively deteriorated, it left a clue for the dating of some of the books. The stages of deterioration, called "A" through "F," are measured by the size and number of breaks in the frame line of the device, for these grow worse with time. The comparison of the states of the device from book to book can, therefore, be used in the endeavor to establish dates.[17]

Early printed books may have uneven right margins because the process for spacing the lines to obtain an even margin was not one which could be learned from the traditional methods of making manuscript books and required a little time to develop. When Caxton's books lack a printed date, the fact that the margins are or are not even may help to date them, for he seems to have acquired the technique of justifying in 1480.

Caxton used a total of ten identifiable fonts of type, 1, 2, 2*, 3, 4, 4*, 5, 6, 7, and 8. Those designated 2* and 4* are modifications of 2 and 4. One font was not discarded when another was secured, and various fonts were sometimes used together; but the general chronology of Caxton's undated books can again be deduced in part by an examination of the first dated occurrence of a given font of type and of other books printed in the same typeface.

Some of the terminology used in describing early books is convenient to have in mind. These books were printed on large sheets, usually of paper, but sometimes of vellum. The sheets were then folded and gathered together to place the pages in proper order. If a sheet is printed on both sides so as to produce four printed pages and is folded down the middle to make two leaves, it is called a *folio*. If the sheet is folded twice and contains eight pages, or four leaves, the book is a *quarto*. If the sheet has three folds, sixteen pages, and eight leaves, the book is an *octavo*. Several sheets folded and inserted within one another are called a *gathering*, or the gathering may be made of one sheet only. It was customary in early printing, as in manuscript books, to mark the sheets that would appear successively in the gathering with a given letter of the alphabet, capital or lower case, and then to add to the letter a sequence of numbers showing the order of leaves in the gathering. This mark, which is called a *signature*, did not need to appear on every page, or even on every leaf, to serve the purposes of enabling the printer to gather the sheets in the correct order. The pattern by which the sheets are collected in the book is called its *collation*.

Nothing remains of Caxton's shop except the books he printed. There is no record of his payroll, and no inventory of his equipment exists. Who designed and cut his type, how many men he employed, how many presses he operated, and how much he could print in a day cannot be ascertained. The aim of this study, however, is to examine, not how, but what Caxton printed, for the content of his books, not the process of their printing, offers the evidence chiefly needed for an understanding of Caxton's role and that of the printed book in fifteenth century England. That Caxton visited Cologne, learned to print, and used what he had learned to produce more than one hundred editions of English incunabula are the facts that really matter.

V   *Caxton's Press at Bruges*

Caxton returned from Cologne to Bruges and printed a few books, presumably with Colard Mansion, a scrivener turned printer. William Blades, one of the first students to provide an extended study of Caxton's printing career, held that Mansion taught Caxton to print; but, though many writers followed Blades in this assertion, the evidence of Caxton's long stay in Cologne has largely dispelled the argument. L. A. Sheppard, who has advanced the view that the Mansion and Caxton presses were separate, claims priority for Caxton's press. That the two men worked together is, however, the usual view, and George Painter suggests that Mansion was "probably . . . a junior partner rather than an employee. . . ."[18]

Of the early books printed in Bruges, exactly which are Caxton's is a nice problem. *The New Cambridge Bibliography of English Literature* lists as Caxton's Bruges books: Raoul Lefèvre, *The Recuyell of the Historyes of Troye*, translated by Caxton; Jacobus de Cessolis, *The Game and Play of the Chess*, translated by Caxton; Pierre d'Ailly, *Septenuaire de pseaulmes de penitence;* Raoul Lefèvre, *Le recueil des histoires de Troyes* (in French); Raoul Lefèvre, *Les fais et proesses du Jason;* Jean Mielot, *Les quatre choses derrenieres* (this title often appears as *Cordiale*, or when the reference is to the English translation, as *Cordial*); and, as either Bruges or Westminster, John Russell, *Propositio clarissimi oratoris magistri Johannis Russell.* George Painter presents the same list except that he assigns the *Propositio . . . Johannis Russell* to Westminster. An older scholar, E. Gordon Duff, makes the Bruges books simply the English translation of *The Recuyell of the Historyes of Troye, The*

Game and Play of the Chess, and *Les quatre choses derrenieres.* [19] The assignment of incunabula to their printers may never be definitively made.

Subject to less argument is the conclusion that from the Bruges days forward Caxton had, or sought, patronage for the publication of some of his books. The remarks about Margaret of Burgundy's encouragement of his work on *The Recuyell of the Historyes of Troye* have to do directly with encouragment to translate, not with patronage of the press. They suggest, nevertheless, the likelihood that Margaret also patronized the printing venture.

The dedication of Caxton's second book, *The Game and Play of the Chess* [1475?], presents a problem in interpretation. [20] Caxton offered the book to a royal sponsor, George, Duke of Clarence, a brother of the Duchess of Burgundy and of Edward IV of England. Since Clarence's reputation suggests that he was noble in blood rather than in character, scholars have presented various possible answers to the question of why Caxton would have dedicated any book, and this book in particular, to him. *The Game and Play of the Chess* explains the chessmen and their moves in terms of human society and assesses the morality of various ways of behaving; it asserts that the analogy it offers was contrived by a philosopher as moral instruction to an evil and oppressive ruler named Evilmerodach who would not listen to direct advice. Why would Caxton have felt that *The Game and Play of the Chess* was appropriate to Clarence?

Caxton's Prologue declares that Clarence needs no instruction in right conduct, for his illustrious reputation "shines as well in strange regions as within the realm of England. . . ." Although Caxton makes it quite clear that he knows Clarence only by reputation, he nevertheless declares his conviction that Clarence is devoted to his brother's realm and to the instruction of the people "in good, virtuous, profitable, and honest manners" and that he will stand sponsor to the book for the "common good" (Crotch, pp. 10, 12). That Caxton really believed Clarence to be a model of nobility is possible but hardly likely; indeed, the implication usually seen in these remarks is that the book was printed in the hope that Clarence, like Evilmerodach, would be beguiled into reform. George Painter has proposed a new and, I think, doubtful reading of the dedication to Clarence as "propaganda for Clarence and criticism of Edward's rule" at a time when Clarence aspired to the throne. [21]

If Clarence's family requested the book in the hope that Clarence would read it and change his evil ways, the family would surely have financed the publication. If Caxton initiated the venture in the hope of reforming Clarence, he might have hoped also to be remunerated by a grateful family. If Painter is correct, Clarence might have remunerated Caxton for the "propaganda." If Caxton simply dedicated a book to a man he did not know and knew too little about, he might have aspired to please and therefore to be rewarded. Whichever of the several suppositions proposed by various scholars (see note 20, above) is correct—and the last is perhaps the least open to objection Clarence pursued his ambitions to the conclusion of death in the Tower of London in 1478, and Caxton dropped the dedication for the second edition of *The Game and Play of the Chess,* printed at Westminster [1482]. He then began the Prologue with a quotation from St. Paul, one already used in *The Recuyell:* "All that is written is written to our doctrine and for our learning" (Crotch, p. 10). Sometimes time supplies the ironies of literature.

VI *Caxton's Press at Westminster*

For reasons which Caxton apparently never recorded, he removed himself and his printing press to Westminster. Documents show that Caxton rented space in the precincts of Westminster Abbey from 1476 until his death in 1491 and that he subsequently, at an uncertain date, acquired additional space over the Almonry Gate.[22] He had a press in operation at Westminster by 1477, when *The Dicts or Sayings of the Philosophers,* translated by Anthony Woodville, Earl Rivers, the brother-in-law of Edward IV, was printed. *The Dicts or Sayings* is the first book with a printed date that was published in England in English. The discovery in 1928 of an indulgence, printed with Caxton's type in Latin and dated by hand December 13, 1476, has often been taken to prove that Caxton was printing at Westminster in 1476.[23] The indulgence refers to the sixth regnal year of Pope Sixtus IV, which began August 25, 1476, when Caxton presumably would have stopped printing in Bruges if he were to occupy the quarters he rented in Westminster as of September 1476. K. Povey, however, argues that the indulgence could have been printed in Bruges in anticipation of the new regnal year.

Establishing beyond dispute the dates of all of Caxton's books is impossible, but some of them do provide a clear record of the date of printing. *The Dicts or Sayings* states: "Here endeth the book named *The Dicts or Sayings of the Philosophers,* enprinted by me William Caxton at Westminster the year of Our Lord .M.CCCC. Lxxvij. . ."

(Crotch, p. 18). Some of Caxton's books give the date of translation rather than of printing. For example, the Epilogue to *The Mirror of the World* carries Caxton's statement—"I began first to translate [this book] the second day of January, the year of Our Lord M.CCCC.lxxx. And finished the viij day of March the same year" (Crotch, p. 59)—and suggests a probable date for the printing as some time in 1480. Other Caxton editions that make no mention of date must be dated inferentially, as we have noted, on the basis of type faces, watermarks on the paper, topical references, probable work schedules, even margins, and the like. Wide discrepancies in the dates argued by various scholars, and even by the same scholar at different times in his study, exist. Because George D. Painter has made a new consideration of the evidence, the dates in the body of this book follow his, though the reader needs to realize that they may not be firm. Painter, who accepts the 1476 indulgence as Westminster work, also suggests that several undated books were printed at Westminster prior to the printing of *The Dicts*—the first editions of three small volumes: Benet Burgh's translation of *Parvus Cato; Magnus Cato*, John Lydgate's *The Churl and the Bird* and his *The Horse, Sheep, and Goose* in 1476, and the one edition of Caxton's translation of Raoul Lefèvre's *Jason* in 1477.[24]

An undated *Advertisement* survives from Caxton's Almonry shop:

If it please any man spiritual or temporal to buy any Pies of two and three commemorations of Salisbury use enprinted after the form of this present letter which been well and truly correct, let him come to Westminster into the Almonry at the red pale and he shall have them good cheap.
Supplico stet cedula[25]

Scholars have made full use of the small clues offered by the *Advertisement*. A *Pie* contains directions for dealing with certain variable elements in the mass. Inferential dating of the *Advertisement* and of the *Pie* to which it refers implies the date for Caxton's occupancy of the Almonry shop—as early as 1479 in Painter's view, or even 1477 in Blake's. The *Advertisement* tells us that Caxton's shop sign was a red pale, an heraldic emblem of the sort used to mark businesses for customers who could not read. The Latin request that the notice not be torn down, *Supplico stet cedula*, may suggest that the passer-by will be able to read Latin.

At Westminster, as at Bruges, Caxton's prologues and epilogues refer to eminent persons, patrons, and friends, and they reveal a good deal about Caxton and the world in which he lived. For example, *The*

History of Jason [1477], like *The Recuyell of the Historyes of Troye* a translation from a French text of Lefèvre's, has a Prologue which states that the book honors the founding of the Order of the Golden Fleece, among whose members is Caxton's "most dread natural liege lord" (Crotch, p. 33), King Edward. Caxton offered the book not to Edward IV, however, but to the young Edward, Prince of Wales, in the hope that he would be led by its novelty to learn to read English. The Prologue suggests that Caxton probably chose and printed the text on his own initiative, and he must have expected that other children, too, would find it an incentive for learning to read.

One of the curious aspects of Caxton's prologues and epilogues is that they have often acquired prophetic or emotional overtones because of later events of history. The young Edward to whom *Jason* was dedicated was one of the princes presumably murdered by their uncle Richard after Edward IV's death, an event in the future which Caxton could not have foreseen but which gives pathos to his prayer that God will "save and increase in virtue" this "our to-coming [future] sovereign lord . . ." (Crotch, p. 34).

Caxton speaks in the Prologue to *Jason* of translating "under the protection and sufferance" (Crotch, p. 33) of Edward IV. The Prohemye to the set of essays, *Of Old Age, Of Friendship, The Declamation of Noblesse* (1481), states that the volume was printed "under the shade and shadow of the noble protection" of Edward (Crotch, p. 44). The Epilogue to *Godfrey of Boloyne,* also printed in 1481, speaks of the printer's wish to "present" it to Edward; and the *Polychronicon* [1482] refers to Edward's protection of the printer. Whether such comments mean that Caxton worked at Westminster under some special protection granted him as a printer[26] or simply that he, like every citizen, had the king's protection, cannot be ascertained. It is possible, however, that Atkyns's story about the first printer's coming to England at the king's express will refers to a genuine tradition but assigns it to the wrong king and to the wrong printer.

In addition to *The Dicts or Sayings of the Philosophers,* Anthony Woodville translated two other texts which Caxton printed, *The Moral Proverbs* of Christine de Pisan (1478) and *The Cordial* (1479). Caxton's biographers believe that Rivers surely assumed responsibility for seeing that the printer did not suffer financially from printing these translations. Since *The Dicts, The Moral Proverbs,* and *The Cordial* are not Caxton's own translations, he did not write prologues for them, but he did supply epilogues for all three. In the Epilogue to

The Cordial, he records a prayer for Rivers that he might have "after this short, dangerous, and transitory life everlasting permanence in heaven . . ." (Crotch, p. 39). When Rivers was executed at the order of Richard III after trying to secure the succession of the dead Edward IV's throne to Edward's son, these words acquired poignant appropriateness.

The Curial, which was originally written in French by Alain Chartier, translated by Caxton, and published by him about 1483, has a Prologue of eight lines and a two line colophon. The Prologue indicates that "a noble and virtuous earl" (Crotch, p. 89) gave Caxton a copy of *The Curial* and requested its translation. *The Curial* is a protest against the vanity, deceit, and malice of the court. If the earl is correctly identified as Rivers,[27] his hand in this particular book now has an ironical significance.

The Prologue to *The Order of Chivalry* [1484] is itself a translation, but the Epilogue attributes Caxton's translating the book to the "request of a gentle and noble esquire" (Crotch, p. 82) who is not named. The Epilogue laments the decay of chivalry from the glorious days of Arthur's knights; of Richard I, Edward I, Edward III and his sons; of Sir Robert Knolles, Sir John Hawkwood, Sir John Chandos, Sir Walter Manny; and of Henry V and his captains; and others. The book was presented to Richard III in the hope that he in turn would urge it upon "lords, knights, and gentlemen" (Crotch, p. 84), who could learn from it the true practice of chivalry and honor.

Although the Epilogue records Caxton's promise to pray for Richard III's "long life & prosperous welfare," for his "victory of all his enemies," and for his "everlasting life in heaven" (Crotch, p. 84), it neglects to praise Richard. The list of English kings who are lauded is long, and the lament for the decay of England clearly implies that England's loss of her place in the world's esteem results from the lack of a leader such as she had enjoyed in King Arthur or in Richard I. Three persons whom Caxton had mentioned in earlier prologues and epilogues—Clarence, Rivers, and the young Prince of Wales—had died, probably as the result of Richard III's ambition, by the time this book was printed. The omission of praise and the implication of blame for Richard III can hardly be read as anything but an indication of Caxton's opinion and his courage. Whatever "noble esquire" requested *The Order of Chivalry*, it was Caxton who set his own name to the translation, to the printing, and to the dedication. In the year following the publication of *The Order of Chivalry*, Richard lost his crown at Bosworth Field. Caxton's

Epilogue seems almost prophetic, and its emotional tone undoubtedly reflects his feeling for the urgency of the reform which he hoped to stimulate by a book on chivalry and honor.[28]

In 1489, Caxton printed a military treatise, Christine de Pisan's *Feats of Arms*, because Henry VII, Richard III's successor, sent him a copy by the hand of the Earl of Oxford with an expression of the royal will that Caxton translate and print it "to the end that every gentleman born to arms & all manner [of] men of war, captains, soldiers, victualers, & all other, should have knowledge how they ought to behave them in the feats of war . . ." (Crotch, p. 103). The praise by Caxton of Henry VII in the Epilogue contrasts pointedly with his failure to praise Richard five years earlier. Nonetheless, Caxton tempers his praise with ambiguity; he calls Henry, who was, after all, the king by right of military conquest, "the highest & most Christian king & prince of the world" because, Caxton says, he has never heard of a prince who "hath subdued his subjects with less hurt . . ." (Crotch, p. 104).

Henry's mother, Margaret Beaufort, Duchess of Somerset, gave Caxton a French manuscript with the command that he translate it into English. Having obeyed, he "presents" her with the book, *Blanchardin and Eglantine* [1488], a prose romance of knights and ladies, courtship and marriage. *Fifteen Oes* [1491], a short series of prayers, was ordered by Henry's mother and his queen, Elizabeth. Chivalry, romance, and religion—the foci of these three books chosen by Henry VII, his mother, and his wife—epitomize upper class Medieval life. Furthermore, Caxton's translation of *Eneydos* [1490?], which is dedicated to Arthur, Prince of Wales and Henry VII's son, seems to represent a characteristic gracious gesture on the part of the old printer to the young prince.

Two of Caxton's Westminster editions speak directly to the issue of remuneration. *The Golden Legend*, of which Caxton's first edition was printed about 1484, has the Prologue that contains his famous lament that the burden of translating and printing so large a work left him "half desperate" because of the time and the money involved; but he added that William, Earl of Arundel, had promised to give him "a yearly fee, that is to wit, a buck in summer & a doe in winter" and also "to take a reasonable quantity of them when they were achieved & accomplished. . . ." Caxton dedicated the book to Arundel with the hope that "it [would] like [please] him to remember my fee . . ." (Crotch, p. 70). Caxton says that he translated and printed the Charlemagne romance, *Four Sons of Aymon* [1488], at the request of

John, Earl of Oxford, his "good, singular, and especial lord . . ." (Crotch, p. 106). The cost was great, and Caxton records, somewhat urgently, his hope for a suitable reward.[29]

Indicative of Caxton's place in the world and of his unruffled acceptance of that place is the fact that he mentions these royal and noble persons in a tone that is little different from his references to persons of less rank. He printed Chaucer's translation of *Boethius de consolatione philosophiae* [1478] at the "request of a singular friend & gossip of mine" (Crotch, p. 37) who is unnamed, and he also translated *The Knight of the Tower* (1484) for an unnamed lady of rank. The Prologue to *The Life of Charles the Great* (1485) records that the text was printed at the "request of my good, singular lords & special masters and friends" (Crotch, p. 97); in the Envoy, William Daubeney is specifically mentioned as having asked Caxton to make the translation. *The Royal Book* [1487] was given to Caxton in French by "a singular friend of mine, a mercer of London . . ." (Crotch, p. 101). *The Book of Good Manners* (1487) was brought to him in French by "An honest man & a special friend of mine, a mercer of London named William Praat" (Crotch, p. 99) since deceased. In printing *The Mirror of the World*, in two editions of about 1481 and about 1489, Caxton recorded that he translated the text "at the request, desire, cost, and dispense of the honorable & worshipful man Hugh Bryce, alderman & citizen of London, intending to present the same unto the virtuous, noble, and puissant lord, William, Lord Hastings" (Crotch, p. 52). This is an especially interesting statement, since it not only indicates patronage but also suggests that the printed book had become a flattering gift, one similar to a presentation copy of a manuscript.

Caxton did not always readily concur when asked to publish a book. "Many noble and diverse gentlemen" (Crotch, p. 92) had to argue the case for the historicity of King Arthur before Caxton consented to print Sir Thomas Malory's *Le Morte d'Arthur* in 1485. In the Prologue to *Eneydos*, Caxton relates that the abbot of Westminster presented him "certain evidences" (of what, Caxton does not say) in an English "more like to Dutch than English" (Crotch, p. 108). He found the material impossible to manage and abandoned the endeavor to print it.

Several conclusions can be drawn from these comments. The precise degree of Caxton's intimacy with the ruling family or others whom he mentions cannot be determined, but Caxton obviously was known to merchants, churchmen, the general nobility, and several of the kings who reigned during his lifetime. He seems to have known Margaret of Burgundy well. That Rivers offered Caxton his translations to print and, in the case of *The Dicts,* to correct suggests some degree of intimacy between Caxton and the king's brother-in-law. Whether all of these persons could properly be called patrons or not, their money was sometimes a factor in the decision to print a book.

The various people mentioned in the prologues and epilogues hardly constituted an editorial board, but they were able to persuade Caxton to print certain texts, even though he occasionally protested. All of them—royalty, nobility, clergy, and merchants—must have believed in the importance of the press as a means of educating readers about facts and about ways of acting. They must also have believed that printed books could have significant effects on the lives of readers and on the welfare of the kingdom. They must have thought that Englishmen needed English books and that many books in other languages were of such value as to necessitate their being "Englished" for potential readers. At Bruges and at Westminster, Caxton was surrounded by people who, like himself, saw something of the power latent in the printing press and encouraged its development.

Nineteen of the thirty-three books for which Caxton wrote prologues and epilogues make some mention of the person or persons who encouraged their printing. To these may be added the somewhat different matter of the second edition of *The Canterbury Tales.* In the Proem to the second edition, published about 1483 (after a first edition without prologue or epilogue about 1478), Caxton says that a gentleman came to him with a complaint about the badness of the text of the first edition and offered him the use of a better manuscript for a new edition. Caxton readily printed the new edition to redress the harm done Geoffrey Chaucer by the faulty text of the first edition.

Of the books which have prologues and epilogues, only seven lack all mention of patronage, protection, or dedication. Scholars[30] have often noted that a number of the books without prologues and epilogues are of a kind likely to sell easily and that several may have been commissioned even though they do not mention sponsors or patrons. About a third of the items in the list of Caxton titles are religious—books of hours and other books of prayers, indulgences, sermons, and so on. These may represent publications requested by the church. Another, *Propositio . . . Johannis Russell,* contains a statement that was made in the year 1470 by John Russell about the Order of the Garter and is assigned a printing date of 1477 or 1478. It is the sort of book which might have been commissioned and paid for, as might the *Statutes of Henry VII* [1490]. The *Statutes*, for the first, third, and fourth regnal years of Henry VII, believed to be the earliest printed statutes of any English king, deal with various topics: trade regulation, landholding, the protection of fish spawning areas, and so on. The editions of two rhetorics, L. G. Traversagni's *Nova rhetorica* [1479] and the abridgement of it called *Epitoma sive isagogicum margarite castigate eloquentie* [1480], and the grammar by Aelius Donatus, revised by Antonio Mancinello and called *Donatus melior* [1487], could have been requested by such an interested party as a school, for example.

Something like two-thirds of Caxton's publications, therefore, may have had a guarantee or a strong implication of financial support from a source other than the casual purchaser. Even if it is assumed that many of these were independently selected by Caxton and published at his own risk, they were suited to reasonably predictable ends and audiences. Indeed, certain other titles may have found a ready sale among Caxton's merchant friends and acquaintances who were seeking instructional texts for their children and apprentices—for example, *The Book of Courtesy* [1477–1478]; *Parvus Cato; Magnus Cato*, in four editions, probably dating between 1476 and 1484; *Vocabulary in French and English* [1480]; and perhaps also *Description of Britain* (1480), *Chronicles of England* (in two editions of 1480 and 1482), and *Polychronicon* [1482]. A brief layman's guide to good health, like *Governal of Health; Medicina stomachi* [1491], might have found many purchasers.

To see Caxton's book selections as indicative of the likelihood that his press was solvent is not to impute blame, but some of his critics have done so. It is, however, to see his work in only a partial light. While the cause of English letters would have been ill-served by Caxton's operating a press so loftily learned as to reach few readers, Caxton in fact did more than serve predictable, pedestrian needs. He printed prose tales in translation, his or Malory's; he indulged heavily in the publication of native English poets—Chaucer, Gower, and Lydgate—for no discernible reason except that he loved them; and he seems to have translated *The Metamorphoses of Ovid*, the anonymous *Reynard the Fox* [1481 and 1488], and *Fables of Aesop* (1484) for the same reason.

VII *Caxton and the Manuscript Book*

Although Caxton printed books and sold them, a few tantalizing scraps of evidence suggest that he also had some part in the manuscript trade.[31] As we have earlier indicated, he learned to print in order to escape from making copies of *The Recuyell;* and his lament at the boredom and fatigue of copying that text suggests that he was not a professional scrivener. *Blanchardin and Eglantine*, the book he translated at the command of Margaret of Somerset, was made from a manuscript which he "had long before sold to my said lady . . ." (Crotch, p. 105), a comment which proves that he sold one manuscript and implies the possibility that he was in the regular business of selling them.

The most interesting evidence concerning Caxton and the manuscript trade, however, rests in his translation of *The Metamorphoses of Ovid*.[32] Among the books Samuel Pepys gave Magdalene College, Cambridge University, in the eighteenth century is a manuscript of Books x–xv of *The Metamorphoses*. The colophon to this fragment of *The Metamorphoses* states that Caxton completed a translation of the full fifteen books on April 22, 1480. In 1964, when Books i–ix of the manuscript were found, one leaf was partly torn away, but the rest was intact. The manuscript of *The Metamorphoses* has been examined meticulously by students of printing, but it has yielded no definitive evidence about Caxton's intention for the book. Many suggestions have been made: that the manuscript was prepared for a compositor to use in setting type—and the countersuggestion that it is much more elaborately designed than a compositor would have required and shows no signs of having been marked by a compositor; that the manuscript was prepared in the hope of securing financial aid toward its printing or as a presentation copy; that the manuscript was made from a printed text which is now lost.

A few remarks in prologues and epilogues offer clues as to the place of *The Metamorphoses* in the overall picture of Caxton's work, but they are inconclusive. The colophon of the Ovid itself declares the translation to be finished, but it makes no statement about printing. The Prologue to *The Golden Legend* lists several books which Caxton had translated, and the inclusion of "the xv books of Metamorphoses" (Crotch, p. 71) among other books which he had both translated and printed suggests that it too was printed. Indeed, to some readers the notice in *The Golden Legend* sounds a bit like an advertisement for the books, and the statement made would have been somewhat excessive if only a manuscript copy or so of one of them were available. If, as has been suggested, the notice was intended as a bid for a sponsor, it was a subtle one; nothing in it indicates that, of the several translations mentioned, one still required a sponsor for its publication. It is hard to believe that Caxton did so much with *The Metamorphoses of Ovid* without going the final step and printing it. Perhaps in an old binding or in an old box somewhere a leaf or even a copy of a printed text still waits to be found. Meanwhile, the manuscript teases the imagination.

In summary, the facts of Caxton's life reveal a well-placed businessman, a wool merchant who turned printer in middle age. Seeking out books, translating them if necessary, printing them, and selling them, Caxton made books his life. To these books, therefore, we need to turn.

CHAPTER 2

Caxton's Scientific and Philosophic Books

SCIENCE and philosophy provide means by which the human race seeks to understand and control its life and environment. Scientific analysis, which was not always fully divorced from superstition, magic, and imagination, was used in the Middle Ages in conjunction with philosophical speculation to reduce the world to a comprehensible scale and to order its diverse parts. A map constructed by drawing a line directly across a circle and a second line across one of the resulting halves and labeling these parts Asia, Africa, and Europe is of little use in practicality; but it puts the world into a simple diagram which can be easily grasped. At the same time, the map leaves the entire obverse of this circle in mysterious blankness.

The Mirror of the World, translated by Caxton and printed by him in 1481, contains such a diagram, and it is followed by another showing Europe, Asia, and Africa on one half of a circle; on the other half appears the backside of the world, labeled *Inhabitabilis*.[1] This "map" makes graphic the unknown world which lurked just outside the flat circle of what Medieval man comprehended about the universe he inhabited. He looked to science, primitive and superstitious as it might be, and to philosophy for an explanation of the order inherent in the chaos which he could readily perceive.

I Scientific-Philosophic Works

Wynkyn de Worde, Caxton's shop foreman, records that Caxton began his career as a printer with a scientific-philosophic treatise, for de Worde says that Caxton learned to print in Cologne by working on an edition, in Latin, of Bartholomaeus Anglicus's *De proprietatibus rerum*, or *The Properties of Things*. This statement appears in de Worde's own edition of an English translation of *De proprietatibus rerum*, printed about 1495. The lines come at the end of the text, but are marked "Prohemium":

And also of your charity call to remembrance,
The soul of William Caxton, first printer of this book,
In Latin tongue at Cologne, himself to advance,
That every well disposed man may thereon look.[2]

Little is known about Bartholomaeus Anglicus beyond his having been an Englishman and a Franciscan friar who wrote the Latin *De proprietatibus* about 1230–1250. John Trevisa completed a translation of Bartholomaeus into English in 1398, the translation which de Worde published. Thomas Berthelet published an English edition in 1535, and in 1582 Thomas East published an English text with a commentary, *Batman upon Bartholome*. The British Museum *Catalogue of Printed Books* contains an extensive list of Latin editions from such a variety of places as Cologne, Basel, Lyons, Nuremberg, Argentine, Heidelberg, Strassburg, and Frankfurt, as well as editions in various vernacular languages.

Edward Grant speaks of *De proprietatibus* as "enormously popular for about three centuries, being translated into Italian, French, English, and Spanish during the fourteenth and fifteenth centuries"; and A. C. Crombie calls it the "most popular work on natural history. . . . " Lynn Thorndike notes the large number of surviving manuscripts, along with translations and printed editions, as evidence of Bartholomaeus's popularity, but he characterizes the book as being not "a specimen of the most advanced medieval scholarship, but rather . . . an illustration of the rough general knowledge which every person with any pretense to culture was then supposed to possess." To John Edwin Wells, Bartholomaeus's material was "interesting, and often amusing."[3]

De proprietatibus rerum is, as Wells says, "interesting, and often amusing," but more importantly, it is clear evidence of the Medieval search for order and meaning. It fuses scientific, political, and artistic materials into one great system which is theologically oriented. Bartholomaeus begins with an examination of the nature of God the Trinity, then of angels and reasonable souls. Heaven and earth, time, matter, air, birds, water, fish, the political divisions of the earth, precious stones, metals, herbs and plants, animals, colors, music, and musical instruments all fall under his purview in the nineteen more or less systematically developed books of *De proprietatibus rerum*.

Nothing suggests that Caxton took an active part in the decision to print *De proprietatibus rerum;* but about a decade after he began as printer, he issued a similar encyclopedic compendium of learning,

The Mirror of the World [1481], which he not only chose to publish but to translate himself in order to make it available to his country-men in their own language. Like *De proprietatibus rerum*, *The Mirror of the World* is a thirteenth century compilation. It exists in two French versions—a poem, *Image du monde*, and a prose piece of the same title translated from the poem. The prose and perhaps the poem were by Gossouin or Gautier de Metz, but Caxton translated from the French prose.[4]

Caxton's Prologue advises why and how the book should be read:

Then whoever will comprise [understand] and understand [Caxton rarely resists the opportunity to use doublets: *comprise* and *understand*] the substance of this present volume, for to learn and know especially the creation of this world, the greatness of the firmament and littleness of the earth in regard of heaven, how the vii sciences were founded and what they be, by which he may the better avail [prosper] in knowledge all the days of his life, then let him read this said volume treatably [carefully], advisedly, and ordinately [properly], that, in such thing as he shall read, he suffer [allow] nothing to pass but that he understand it right well; and so may he know and understand veritably the declaration of this said volume. And he then that so will obey this commandment may, by the content of the same, learn great part of the form and condition of this world, and how, by the will of Our Lord, it was by Him created, made, and accomplished, and the cause wherefore it was established; whereof the debonair Lord hath done to us so great grace that we ever been bound to give him laud and worship, or else we had not been of any value nor worth any thing, no more than unreasonable beasts.[5]

Chapter I "treateth first of the power and puissance of God" (p. 8), a theological explanation of the nature and power of God. Chapters II, III, and IV concern "Wherefore God made and created the world" (p. 11), "Wherefore God formed man like unto his image and to his semblance" (p. 12), and "Wherefore God made not the man such as he might not sin" (p. 14). In his twenty years as printer, Caxton offered the public a variety of material, some of it lacking profundity or serious purpose; but, however vain and idle a few of Caxton's publications were, the world for which he published was firmly established in a theology that governed its approach to the question of how and why man and the world were created. The opening chapters of *The Mirror of the World* indicate exactly where the Middle Ages stood to view itself.

Having begun with a theological account of the creation and of man's role in the universe, *The Mirror* moves to the subject of

"Wherefore and how the vii Artes liberal were founded and of their order" (p. 19). Chapter V begins:

Now declareth this book which is drawn out of Astronomy how sometime [at some time] the notable and wise philosophers would inquire of the manner of the world, and how it had been created and made of God, whereof much people marveled.

And then when the world was made and compassed, there was people enough of which many beheld the firmament that turned round about the world and moved. They had great marvel how it might be made, and they waked and studied many nights and many days. Then began they to behold the stars that rose in the east, and moved about over their heads. (p. 19)

One inescapable observation to be made about these paragraphs is that their opening premise, that the world was made by God, establishes anew that the book reposes solidly on the theological position of the opening chapters. But also significant is the fact that the observers with whom *The Mirror of the World* is concerned are called philosophers. Science, defined as a "particular branch of knowledge or study; a recognized department of learning," is recorded in *The Oxford English Dictionary* from the fourteenth century, with the comment that "In the Middle Ages 'the seven (liberal) sciences' was often used synonymously with 'the seven liberal arts', for the group of studies comprised by the *Trivium* (Grammar, Logic, Rhetoric) and the *Quadrivium* (Arithmetic, Music, Geometry, Astronomy)."[6] *The Mirror of the World*, as we shall see shortly, takes precisely this approach to science: it is analyzed as seven liberal arts.

Although the word science is Medieval, scientist is not documented in *The Oxford English Dictionary* until 1840. Philosopher is used in the Middle Ages in the broadest sense of "a lover of wisdom." It can be rather generously expanded to include rank charlatans like the "old philosopher" who in Chaucer's *Franklin's Tale* creates the illusion that certain black rocks along the coast of Brittany have disappeared, a feat undertaken for the purpose of enabling a young squire to compel a knight's wife to become his mistress. In Ranulf Higden's *Polychronicon* (see Chapter 3, below), necromancer and philosopher are used synonymously to describe Virgil.

The philosophers of *The Mirror of the World*, however, are characterized in the paragraphs immediately following those quoted above as ascetics whose lifestyle is much like that of the church fathers who meditated in their cells or in desert wastes:

Certainly these philosophers apetyted [sought, desired] not these great mangeries [banquets] nor delicious wines, nor for to fill their bellies as do beasts that seek nothing but their pasture, like as in this day do they that retch of [reck, heed, care for] nothing but to fill their paunch with good wines and good victuals and after to have a fair bed, white sheets and soft, and there to sleep like the swine [swine sleeping on soft white sheets is poetic license]. But those were waking and studying many nights, and it grieved them not; but they were embellished much [greatly cheered, *The Oxford English Dictionary* cites this passage from Caxton as its sole example of *embellish* in the figurative sense of "brighten (in feeling), cheer"] of that [because] they saw the firmament thus turn and so nobly to hold his course and terms. (p. 19)

The Mirror's description of unworthy workers sounds remarkably like John Milton's famous digression in "Lycidas" about unworthy churchmen who

> for their bellies' sake
> Creep and intrude and climb into the fold!
> Of other care they little reck'ning make
> Than how to scramble at the shearer's feast. . . .[7]

The philosophers in *The Mirror of the World* have used the method of direct observation to arrive at the mistaken "fact" that the heavens encircle the earth and that all the universe rotates around our little world as center: "Then began they to behold the stars that rose in the east, and moved about over their heads" (p. 19). Ptolemy's name appears only toward the end of *The Mirror*, but the basic conception of the structure of the universe it employs is Ptolemaic and rests on the assumption that what we see exists; we stand in the middle and all that moves moves around us. Copernicus proved Ptolemy wrong about the organization of the universe, but no one has proved *The Mirror* and its philosophers wrong about the grandeur of the heavens as they sweep above the silent observer. Although we can find faults with Medieval lore, we need to be cautious about allowing our own greater science to blind us to what Medieval man actually saw when he looked and was unaided by superciliousness.

The Mirror of the World states explicity what the end of knowledge is:

And therefore the ancient fathers would employ them[selves] and assay the works of Our Lord, and first for to have knowledge of his power and his virtue, considering that they might not occupy themself in a more digne [worthy] nor worthy science nor more difficult. And when the more that they knew of his works and of his wisdom, so much more had they the better will to love their creator and maker and to honor him, considering that he made so noble a thing and so worthy as is the heaven in which been the stars that shine bright therein, and his other marvellous virtues which they praised much . . . . (p. 22)

Chapter VI of *The Mirror of the World* begins with a discussion "Of three manner [kinds] of people":

The philosophers that then were, and which that ought to teach and learn others, accounted only three manner of people in the world after their understanding: and that [those] were clerks, knights, and laborers. The laborers ought to purvey for the clerks and knights such things as were needful for them to live by in the world honestly; and the knights ought to defend the clerks and the laborers, [so] that there were no wrong done to them; and the clerks ought to enseigne [ensign: teach; *The Oxford English Dictionary* shows various passages in Caxton, in his translations of *Jason, The Golden Legend,* and *The Game and Play of the Chess,* as its earliest examples of ensign in the two meanings, "to point out" and "to instruct"] and teach these ii manner of people, and to address them in their works in such wise that none do things by which he should displease God nor lose his grace. (pp. 29–30)

Thus the entire human race and its social structure are reduced to three simply defined classes, the traditional "three estates." Such a formula, repeated at least from King Alfred's time, speaks to a deep need for pattern, order, and stability, and appears frequently in the books Caxton printed.

Higden's *Polychronicon,* Book II, Chapter 33, folio Cx, r, offers an account of the origins of philosophy:

In Romulus' time was Tales Millesius [Thales of Miletus] in his flowers, the first of the seven wise men . . . .

This Tales was the first that searched natural philosophy, causes and working of heaven, kind [nature] of things; and afterward Plato departed [divided] his doing in four, in arithmetic, geometry, music, and astronomy.

This natural philosopher and diviner searched kind [nature] and virtues of things and warned and told before [in advance] the eclipses of the sun and of the moon, and he trowed [believed] that moisture is the beginning of all things, and men sayeth that he lived in the lxviij Olympiad.

(To discover how close the twentieth century is to the facts of the fourteenth and fifteenth, we could compare Higden's statement on Thales to the entry in *Webster's Biographical Dictionary*, 1963).

With Chapter VII, *The Mirror of the World* moves into a set of short chapters defining the liberal arts—the three members of the Trivium: Grammar, Logic, and Rhetoric; and the four members of the Quadrivium: Arithmetic, Geometry, Music, and Astronomy. When Grammar is defined as "the science to form the speech" (p. 34), we are told that "God made the world by words" (p. 34) and that grammar is "the foundation and the beginning of clergy [learning]" (p. 33). Rhetoric can be instrumental in man's salvation; it teaches right and wrong; and "to do wrong to another, whoso doth it, is lost and damned, and for to do right and reason to every man, he is saved and getteth the love of God his creator" (p. 36). Arithmetic teaches "the ordinance of all things," and "By ordinance was the world made and created, and by ordinance of the Sovereign it shall be defeated [destroyed]" (p. 37). As for astronomy, it is both the first and the last of the liberal arts. It "is of all clergy the end"; by astronomy "were first emprysed [undertaken] and gotten all other sciences"; and whoever "knoweth well and understandeth astronomy, he can set reason in all things . . ." (p. 40). In astronomy, we can find the summation of all the values of a knowledge of the seven liberal arts.

Three matters in *The Mirror's* analysis of the liberal arts require comment. First, the orientation is obviously religious; for both the character and the purpose of learning are posited in religion. Under music we are told: "And this is the very reason why these arts all VII been called VII sciences liberal, for they make the soul liberal [free] and deliver it from all evil" (p. 39). Second, the seven liberal arts are described in such a way as to show them to be keys to the creation and organization of the universe; they are a means toward discovering and comprehending the unity and form of the universe. Third, the pattern of organizing learning into two neat groups with three and four parts each, respectively, provides a tidy, easily mastered formula by which man may the more readily learn his lessons.

The significance of *The Mirror's* analysis of the liberal arts to an understanding of the Medieval point of view cannot be overstressed. In particular, the comments on grammar, rhetoric, and word are

important to the understanding of Caxton. The chief purpose of
Caxton's work as a printer—one stated and restated in the prologues
and epilogues—was to give language permanence and to make
written material available to all readers and hearers for the purpose of
instructing them and of directing them to salvation.

The Mirror of the World proceeds from the liberal arts to the
creation and structure of the universe, and a number of diagrams
illustrate that the universe is formed of four elements—earth, air,
fire, and water—that it is round in shape; and that it contains our
planet earth in the precise center. Both the scientific orientation and
the effort at orderly analysis of an orderly system give way to another
manifest characteristic of the Medieval mind—gullible curiosity. As
the text moves into the geography of the world, accounts of curious
creatures—human and animal, beast, bird, and fish—are heaped one
upon the other in rapid succession, and are also mixed with geo-
graphical information.

The limitations of Medieval experience account in part for
Medieval gullibility. In Part 2, Chapter xiiii, "Of diversities that been
in Europe and in Africa," *The Mirror of the World* states: "In another
isle of Iceland the night endureth vi months and then cometh the day
that dureth other vi months shining fair and clear" (p. 98). The
Medieval reader who had never experienced the long days and nights
of the far north and who had little access to scientific evidence would
surely have found this explanation a marvel and would have accepted
it on faith in much the same way that he would have accepted Chapter
xv, "Of the manner and condition of beasts of these countries," which
states that "If the toad, crapault, or spyncop [spider] bite a man or
woman, they be in danger for to die; it hath been often seen" and that
"The spittle of a man fasting slayeth commonly the spyncop & the
toad if it touch them" (p. 100). There is enough truth in the statement
about the poisonous nature of toads and spiders to lend credence to
the whole generalization. That a fasting man could kill toads and
spiders by spitting on them could have been tested, but the compiler
and the translator of *The Mirror* have apparently been satisfied to
accept an unverified statement.

Again, what could seem more improbable than this statement,
except that we know it to be true: "The spider or spyncop of his
proper nature spinneth and weaveth of his entrails the thread of
which he maketh his nets for to take flies which he eateth" (p. 101).
But immediately following occurs a passage of which the latter half is
not in Caxton's Old French text:[8] "When the sheep hath two whelps

or fawns, she loveth that one much better than that other. She beareth him that she loveth best in her arms, and that other she letteth go, which, when she is hunted, leapeth on the mother's back and holdeth her fast. And that other that she beareth in her arms, she letteth fall and is often constrained to save her self" (p. 101). We can imagine a cartoon in which a sheep carries a lamb in her "arms," but we have difficulty imagining a Medieval shepherd imagining that he has seen such a sight in the pastures of France or England. Yet *The Mirror* argues for the credibility of its material: "Of these things and of many other much people marvel that never heard of such things to fore [before], nor know not thereof as we do here that daily find it, for in this book we find many things and reasons whereof men marvel strongly that never have seen, learned, nor heard of them" (p. 104).

The science of *The Mirror of the World* is, in fact, the science of the poetic imagination or of the artist. The concentric spheres of the universe and the elements of earth, air, fire, and water have produced a body of metaphor out of which the imagination projects an explanation of the relationship of man to the universe, even in the twentieth century. Similarly, the strange fish, flesh, and fowl provide a legacy of metaphor and allegory which realizes itself in art. When we read the description of the unicorn, we are amused by the quaint "unnatural natural history":

> Yet is there another beast of much fair corsage [*The Oxford English Dictionary* cites this passage as its first example of *corsage* meaning "of bodily shape"; doublets are common in Caxton; the doublet stated as here, in definition, is unusual] or shape of body which is called monoceros, which hath the body of an horse and feet of an Olyfant [elephant], head of an hart and voice clear and high & a great tail. And hath but one horn which is in the middle of his forehead, which is four foot long, right [straight] & sharp like a sword and cutting like a razor. And all that he attenyneth [strikes; *The Oxford English Dictionary* cites as its first example of *attain* in this sense Caxton's *Jason*] to fore [before] him and toucheth is broken and cut. And for truth this beast is of such condition that, by whatsomever engine he is taken, of great disdain [anger] he suffreth to be slain and die. But he may not be taken but by a pure virgin which is set to fore him where he shall pass, the which must be well and gently arrayed. Then cometh the beast unto the maid much [very] simply, & sleepeth in her lap. And so he is taken sleeping. (p. 74)

Although this description of the unicorn provides an archetype by means of which poetry and painting make significant statements, we read it, or read *The Mirror*'s account of a great fish with a smile for the naiveté of the story:

In this sea of India is another fish so huge and great that on his back groweth earth and grass; and seemeth properly that it is a great Isle. Whereof it happeneth sometime that the mariners sailing by this sea been greatly deceived and abused, for they wene [believe] certainly that it be firm land; wherefore they go out of their ships thereon. And when they have made their preparations and their lodgings thereon, and lighted their fire and made it to burn after [according to] their need, believing to be on a firm land; but incontinent [immediately] as this marvellous fish feeleth the heat of the fire, he moveth him suddenly and develeth [dives] down into the water as deep as he may. And thus all that is upon him is lost in the sea. And by this means, many ships been drowned and perished, and the people, when they supposed [themselves] to have be in safety. (pp. 88–89)

But hear the story when Milton uses it:

> Thus Satan talking to his nearest mate
> With head uplift above the wave, and eyes
> That sparkling blazed; his other parts besides
> Prone on the flood, extended long and large
> Lay floating many a rood, in bulk as huge
> As whom the fables name of monstrous size,
> . . . .
> . . . . or that sea-beast
> Leviathan, which God of all his works
> Created hughest that swim th'ocean stream;
> Him haply slumb'ring on the Norway foam,
> The pilot of some small night-foundered skiff,
> Deeming some island, oft, as seamen tell,
> With fixèd anchor in his scaly rind
> Moors by his side under the lee, while night
> Invests the sea, and wishèd morn delays:
> So stretched out hugh in length the Arch-Fiend lay
> Chained on the burning lake. . . .[9]

A curious limitation in *The Mirror of the World* arises from a struggle after factuality and accuracy which submerges the metaphorical extensions of some of its tales of marvels. Caxton's prologues and epilogues show that he is aware of a truth which arises from and transcends factual untruth (see Chapter 6, below); but *The Mirror of the World* has deprived itself of this level of truth. *The Mirror* states that lions sleep with their eyes open and brush away their tracks with their tails when pursued. In the bestiary tradition, these facts have meaning; T.H. White's translation of a twelfth century Latin bestiary gives an explanation of the hidden track:

It was in this way that our Saviour . . . once hid the spoor of his love in the high places, until, being sent by the Father, he came down into the womb of the Virgin Mary and saved the human race which had perished. Ignorant of the fact that his spoor could be concealed, the Devil (i.e. the hunter of humankind) dared to pursue him with temptations like a mere man. Even the angels themselves who were on high, not recognizing his spoor, said to those who were going up with him when he ascended to his reward: 'Who is this King of Glory?'

Concerning the open eyes, again in White's translation, the old bestiary tradition explains: "In this very way, Our Lord also, while sleeping in the body, was buried after being crucified—yet his Godhead was awake. As it is said in the *Song of Songs*, 'I am asleep and my heart is awake,' or, in the Psalm, 'Behold, he that keepeth Israel shall neither slumber nor sleep.' "[10]

The Mirror, in treating the matter of symbolism as the matter of science, has undergone a loss, but *The Mirror* argues for the credibility of its accounts:

And be not admeruaylled [astonished] of such things as ye have founden written in this present book, the which may seem to you much [very] strange, diverse, & much difficult to believe, for Our Lord God, which is almighty maker & creator of all things, & in whom all goods & virtues been, hath made by His only will & pleasure in the earth many marvels & many works to be marvelled on, by cause that no man knoweth by no way the reasons wherefore, & therefore we ought not to misbelieve in no wise that we hear read nor told of the marvels of the world unto the time we know it be so or no. . . . (p. 96)

The desire for pattern and order which so characterizes the Middle Ages governs *The Mirror of the World*, as can be seen in its discussion of the value of the invention of horologes or clocks and of the establishment of a system which produces a calendar. *The Mirror*, which also offers a significant statement of the motive behind the search for measurable order, asserts that clocks provide for a well-regulated observance of divine hours, which is pleasing to God, as a well-regulated life is beneficial not only to man's soul but to his bodily health as well:

And men serve God the better in due time, and fare the better and live the longer; for if they ruled so themself to pray at a certain hour, and at an other hour in like wise to eat, and other things in his right hour, it should be a light thing to do and please God if men would apply them as well to such things as they do to do that which confoundeth and slayeth them; that is to wit that they be all inclined to conquer the richesses, of which they cease not night nor day, and wenen [believe] to prolong their life thereby. But they amass and get great treasures and purchase their death. (pp. 150–51)

As it draws to a close, *The Mirror of the World* turns again to the art of astronomy as the key to all knowledge: "All thing is known by Astronomy, save such thing as God will that it be not known. And so it is better to learn that, than to learn to amass and gather together great treasures. For who that coude [knew] Astronomy properly, he should have all that he would have on earth; for him should fail nothing, whatsomever he would and yet more" (p. 161).

From beginning to end, *The Mirror* calls seekers after knowledge, in whatever field, philosophers. Philosophy is finally defined:

But by cause that many times we have spoken of philosophy . . . therefore we shall tell to you what it signifieth. . . . Verray [true] Philosophy is to have knowledge of God and fine love of sapience and to know the secrets and ordinances of divine things and of human, for to know God and his power and what a man ought to be, so that he might conduct him that it might be to God agreeable. Who that well knew God and his mysteries, he should well conne [know] entirely philosophy.

All they been good philosophers that of them self have knowledge. (pp. 166–67)

The essential basis of Medieval thought is stated in two passages at the end of *The Mirror*. One defines mortal life: "And all we shall come more shortly than we would to nought, for this world passeth from time to time like as the wind, & faileth from day to day, & maketh to everych [everyone] a little sojourneying; for it is so full of vanity that there is but little truth therein. And it happeth oftimes that he that weneth longest to sojourn here is he that least while abideth & that soonest taketh his end" (p. 183). The other defines immortal life:

there [in Heaven] is the life perdurable, and there is the perfect and inestimable Joy that ever was and ever shall be. There is every thing established and certain for ever more, without end and without beginning, nor never shall fail; nor there shall never be any doubtaunce [doubt, fear] of death, nor of malady, or sorrow, or anguish, nor of dread, of anger, of travail, of pain, nor of poverty or catiffness [wretchedness], nor of any tribulation that ever may hap in any manner of the world to him that shall have his mansion in heaven. But he shall be continually in joy, in solace, in all delights, and in all goods perdurable and without end. And he shall have more consolation than any man can think or esteem, though he employ all his engien [wit, talent] for to understand it. (pp. 179–81)

Caxton did not compose the matter of *The Mirror of the World*. He was asked by Hugh Bryce to translate it, so that it could be presented to Lord Hastings; he did so, and printed it twice. The book's being this sort of joint enterprise testifies to the fact that it represents the interests and beliefs of Caxton and his world.

II *Other Philosophical and Proverbial Works*

William Caxton was not himself a philosopher; but from certain of the books he published, most conspicuously *The Mirror of the World*, we can deduce the general philosophical and theoretical position of both the man and his age. Most of the works to be discussed in the remainder of this chapter are manuals of practical advice which differ little from the proverbial lore of the folk tradition. Only one, in fact, *Boethius de consolatione philosophiae*, is a serious philosophical treatise.

The "author" of *Parvus Cato; Magnus Cato* appears to be a fiction,[11] but he is one of the best-known authors of the Medieval world, and his little book was used extensively to teach both Latin and morality. After Caxton had printed three editions of the translation of *Parvus Cato; Magnus Cato* that was made by Benet Burgh [1476, 1477 or 1478, 1482], he published a translation of his own from a French text which includes extensive commentary [1484]. The Prologue to the fourth edition dedicates it "unto the noble, ancient, and renowned city, the city of London in England" and recommends the book to school children and to "people of every age" because the present generations lack the virtues of their fathers—in particular, the virtue of acquiring and keeping money (Crotch, p. 77).

The advice in *Cato* is general. The reader is directed to reverence God, father, mother, and wise men; to fear the master; to love the wife; to speak pleasantly; to avoid marriage; to avoid sloth, wickedness, and the wicked; to read good books; to avoid dice; to covet nothing; to say little; to love all men. It forbids too much inquiry into the mysteries of God and enjoins an unremitting fear of death. *Cato* stresses the changefulness of fortune and the dangers of relying on magic and sorcery and declares that dreams have no prophetic value but are the products of overeating and similar causes. The comments range from the nature of the soul to the ill wisdom of marrying a woman for her money, but the culminating advice is to avoid "wanhope" or despair and to cling to hope in adversity, for man should not be without hope as long as he is able to breathe.

In 1477, Anthony Woodville, Earl Rivers, asked Caxton to correct and print Rivers's translation of *The Dicts or Sayings of the Philosophers.* Rivers's Prologue preserves a poignant statement concerning Fortune from a man who was to know even more personally in the future about that lady's vagaries. Rivers declares that every man may expect with certainty to be buffeted by fortune as he has been, "largely & in many different manners. . . ." However, sustained in adversity by reliance on God, Rivers undertook a pilgrimage to the shrine of St. James in Spain in the year 1473. While on shipboard, he read a book which had been translated from the French and found "a glorious fair mirror to all good Christian people" in "the wholesome and sweet sayings of the pagans." He therefore made an English translation, so that his countrymen might similarly benefit from the wisdom of *The Dicts or Sayings of the Philosophers.* [12]

The Dicts is a miscellany of advice about how to treat friends and enemies, about truth and falsehood, about how to govern well, how to conduct a war, how to oversee the copying of one's letters, how to treat malefactors, and so on. Because Caxton printed the book three times, in 1477, [1480] and [1489], *The Dicts* seems to testify to the taste of the century for wholesome but not very profound advice.

Caxton printed a second translation by Rivers, Christine de Pisan's *Moral Proverbs,* in 1478. The similarity of *The Dicts* and the *Proverbs* in intellectual level and in their general format, the scrapbook collection of bits of advice, is marked. *Moral Proverbs* is in verse and runs to a total of four leaves. It begins:

> The great virtues of our elders notable
> Oft to remember is thing profitable.

It ends:

> There is no thing so rich I you ensure [assure]
> As the service of God our creator.
> Little availeth good example to see
> For him that will not the contrary flee.
> Though that the death to us be lamentable
> Hit to remember is thing most convenable [proper].

> Th'end doth show every work as hit is;
> Woe may he be that to God endeth miss [amiss, wrong].
> Explicit[13]

Caxton, or perhaps Rivers and Caxton, added two rime royal stanzas at the end of the text; and, although these have been quoted endlessly, they bear repetition:

> Of these sayings Christine was authoress
> Which in making had such intelligence
> That thereof she was mirror & mistress;
> Her works testify th'experience.
> In French language was written this sentence [maxim]
> And thus Englished doth hit rehearse
> Antoine Woodville, th'Earl Rivers.
>
> Go thou, little quire, and recommend me
> Unto the good grace of my special lord
> Th'Earl Rivers; for I have enprinted thee
> At his commandment, following every word
> His copy, as his secretary can record,
> At Westminster, of February the .xx. day
> And of King Edward the .xvii. year vray [truly].
> Enprinted by Caxton
> In February, the cold season (Crotch, p. 32)

Another work of Christine's, *Feats of Arms,* translated and printed by Caxton (1489), offers more evidence of Christine's right to fame than does her slender volume of *Proverbs,* but she is little known to English readers today.

On August 12, 1481, Caxton printed a set of three essays: two translations from Cicero (or Tully, Tullius), *Of Old Age* (*De senectute*) and *Of Friendship* (*De amicitia*); and *The Declamation of Noblesse* by Bonaccursius de Montemagno. Caxton violates a kind of natural order in the essays: *Of Noblesse* and *Of Friendship* would seem logically to precede rather than follow *Of Old Age;* but the order Caxton uses allows him to put first the essay which makes the central point of the entire group: that mortal life should be lived with a view to living eternally.

Cicero argues in *Of Old Age* that every age, from childhood onwards, has its appropriate characteristics; for, just as "cruelty is appropriate to the age of youth, worshipfulness [distinction] and

sadness [sobriety] of manners be appropriate to the age of viril-
ity. . . . Moderation and temperance be appropriate to old age"; but
all mortal life should be lived so as to achieve eternal life:

the soul is celestial and descended from an high place, and the body is earthly
low and puissant [limited to earthly puissance or strength]. . . .

But I believe that the undeadly gods have spread and sown the souls within
the bodies of mankind to the intent that the men should see and inhabit the
countries, and by cause also that the men considering the ordinances of the
celestial things should follow that ordinance by manner and stableness of life,
that is, to wit, that God which is undeadly hath put and putteth the undeadly
souls within the bodies of the deadly men to the intent that they perceive and
inhabit within this low world to such an end that they consider the ordinance
of heaven and that they may live after [a] stable life, celestial and perdurable
with God.[14]

Caxton then, according to his own statement in the Epilogue to
Tullius of Friendship, added that essay as an appropriate companion
piece to *Of Old Age*: "Then when I had enprinted the book *Of Old
Age*, which the said Tullius made, me seemed it according [it seemed
appropriate to me] that this said book *Of Friendship* should follow by
cause there cannot be annexed to old age a better thing than good and
true friendship." Caxton asserts that the two essays are "full necessary, behoveful, and requisite unto every age, estate, and degree"
and prays that "we may attain after this short, transitory life the
eternal blessed life in heaven, where is joy and glory without end.
Amen" (Crotch, pp. 45–46). *Of Friendship* was written to explain to
two sons-in-law of a Roman senator, Lelius, the friendship which
existed between the late Lelius and Scipio Africanus.

Of Noblesse takes the form of a debate between two young men
who wish to marry a young lady; and each makes his claim to the lady's
hand on the basis of his *noblesse:* in the one case, a matter of family
and wealth; in the other, of personal character. The outcome is not
stated, though that character outweighs blood and money is implied.
Chaucer makes high comedy out of this sort of debate in *The
Parliament of Fowls*, where three tercel eagles of various degrees of
nobility attempt to win a formel eagle by explaining the quality of
their love; in the end, the lady's decision is to delay her answer for a
year. That the Middle Ages could joke about its serious concerns,
however, does not diminish the importance of these topics.

Among Caxton's works which stand in about the same relation to
philosophy as does *Poor Richard's Almanack*, or, to take an example

from Caxton's world, the *Fables of Aesop*, there is one piece of primary importance to Medieval thinkers—*Boethius de consolatione philosophiae* [1478]. Caxton may have chosen Boethius because he was drawn to Boethius himself or to the translator, Chaucer, or simply because he was asked to publish the book. At any rate, he provided readers with a treatise on man's role in the universe which is still considered of primary importance.

Boethius de consolatione philosophiae, along with Chaucer's *Troilus and Criseyde* and *The Monk's Tale* from *The Canterbury Tales*, provides the best summation available of the Medieval view of tragedy, which the Middle Ages did not consider to be a genre, but a theme. Like Earl Rivers, Boethius is a historical person who enjoyed fame, prosperity, and personal happiness before he fell into political disfavor and was imprisoned and executed. While in prison, he debates in *De consolatione* the question of why a good man suffers. The *de casibus*, or "fall of princes," theory of tragedy analyzes tragedy simply: A man in high position is overthrown by fortune; and, from great estate and happiness, he falls to low estate and suffering. In terms of this definition, Boethius himself is a tragic figure. Indeed, blind fortune, who tosses man up and down (like a bucket in a well, says Chaucer's knight) as her wheel spins capriciously round, is a favorite Medieval representation of man's tragedy. The *de casibus* theory functions only for a point of view oriented toward the temporal world, however. Lady Philosophy explains to Boethius that, if he values this slippery world, he will suffer from changing fortune. But, if he values eternity, if he is concerned only with the central issue of his soul's welfare and makes his will completely harmonious with the divine will, the things of this world cannot touch him.

That Caxton shared the view expressed in *The Mirror of the World*, in *Moral Proverbs*, in *Of Old Age*, and in *Boethius de consolatione philosophiae* that mortal life should be conducted in such a way as to lead to a life of eternal happiness is evident in his prologues and epilogues, which endlessly repeat the hope that he expressed in the Epilogue to *Godfrey of Boloyne* that "we might deserve after this present short and transitory life the celestial life to dwell in heaven eternally in joy without end, Amen" (Crotch, p. 48). This statement expresses a central concept in Medieval thinking.

CHAPTER 3

Caxton's Chronicle Histories

MEDIEVAL science and philosophy seek to demonstrate order, truth, and stability, although science in particular cannot always resist a counterproclivity toward the encyclopedic collection of miscellaneous and unverified data. Medieval history stresses continuity; it seeks to be comprehensive; it seeks to state facts. But it is perhaps characterized most markedly, at least at the surface level, by its tendency to be indiscriminate and unpatterned.

I Caxton's Edition of Ranulf Higden's Polychronicon

In 1482 Caxton printed Ranulf Higden's *Polychronicon*. Higden, who died in 1364, wrote the *Polychronicon* or "universal history" in Latin; John Trevisa translated it into English in the 1380s; William Caxton modernized Trevisa's text and added a continuation, Book 8, which brings the material forward to 1461. Caxton's Prologue says that his continuation of history was to 1460, but scholars note that, since Edward IV's accession occurred in 1461 and is discussed in the addition, Caxton's date is in error. Scholars themselves perhaps have been in error in speaking of the continuations of both the *Polychronicon* and the *Chronicles of England* as Caxton's compositions, but precisely where we may begin to speak of "composition" is difficult to define. George D. Painter says that Caxton "reproduced *Chronicles of England* from a manuscript which already contained this continuation, and reprinted much the same text in *Polycronicon,* with a few editorial additions which he took from other sources but did not write himself."[1]

The *Polychronicon* testifies to the Medieval belief in the value of history and of education, and Trevisa's preface to his translation of *Polychronicon* is a lively argument in support of the case for written records and for translations into the vernacular. Trevisa cites the biblical story of the Tower of Babel as a record of the development of a diversity of human languages:

Since the time that the great and high tower of Babylon was builded men have spoken with diverse tongues in such wise that diverse men be strange to other and understand not others' speech. Speech is not known but if [unless] it be learned. Common learning of speech is by hearing & so alway he that is deaf is alway dumb for he may not hear speech for to learn. So men of far countries and lands have diverse speeches; if neither of them have learned other's language, neither of them knows what other meaneth, though they meet and have great need of information and of lore of talking and of speech; be the need never so great neither of them understandeth other's speech no more than gaggling of geese. For jangle that one never so fast that other is never the wiser though he shrew [curse] him instead of good morrow. (folio i, r)

Trevisa knows two remedies for the problem of the lack of a universal language: some men know many tongues, and Latin constitutes a kind of universal tongue. Trevisa then records a dialogue between a lord, identified as Thomas, Earl of Berkeley, and a clerk, Trevisa himself. When the clerk argues that everyone could learn Latin, the lord replies: " 'Not all. For some may not for other manner [kinds of] business, some for age, some for default of wit, some for default of cattle [wealth] or for friends to find them to school [to provide means for them to go to school], and some for other diverse defaults and lets [hindrances]' " (folio i, v). Yet Ranulf Higden, who wrote in Latin because it is widely understood, provides in his book " 'great and noble information and lore to them that can therein read and understand. Therefore I would have these books of Chronicles translated out of Latin into English for [so that] the more men should them understand and have thereof cunning information and lore' " (folio i, r).

To the clerk's reply that a man who knows no Latin may ask another what the book contains, the lord replies that an unlearned man does not know what to ask. Furthermore, not all men who know Latin possess copies of Higden's work, and some who own Higden and can read the Latin lack either the time or the will to tell others what the book contains. The clerk argues: " 'The Latin is both good and fair; therefore it needeth not to have an English translation.' " The lord replies: " 'This reason is worthy to be plunged in a puddle' " and reminds the clerk that the Bible has been translated and that sermons drawn from the Latin Bible are preached in English. He insists that an oral translation will not suffice; it must be written down and preserved. He grants that a translation made by a "lewd" (unlearned) man—presumably such a one as Trevisa—will not be perfect, but he is adamant that it must be made. The clerk surrenders and agrees to prepare the translation (folios i, r-ii, r).

The arguments advanced here for the utility of the written word and for the translation of learned tongues into the vernacular for the common use of the common reader are those which Caxton employs in several of his own prologues; and he operated the press for exactly the end described here, to make useful knowledge available in the common tongue. In fact, Caxton's own Proem to the *Polychronicon* speaks of the value of historical writing: "Great thankings, laud, and honor we meritoriously [in order that we may acquire merit] be bound to yield and offer unto writers of histories, which greatly have profited our mortal life, that show unto the readers and hearers by the examples of things passed what thing is to be desired and what is to be eschewed [avoided]" (Crotch, p. 64). Caxton then proceeds to a definition of history:

History is a perpetual conservatrix of those things that have been done before this present time and also a cotidian [daily] witness of bienfayttes [good feats], of malefaytes [evil feats], great acts and triumphal victories of all manner people. And also if the terrible feigned fables of poets have much stirred and moved men to pity and conserving of justice, how much more is to be supposed that history, assertrix of verity and as mother of all philosophy, moving our manners to virtue, reformeth and reconcileth near hand [almost] all those men which through the infirmity of our mortal nature hath led the most part of their life in ocyosyte [idleness; *The Oxford English Dictionary* gives as its first example of "otiosity" as an English word Caxton's *Caton* of 1483] and misspended their time, passed right soon out of remembrance, of which [of whom] life and death is equal oblivion. The fruits of virtue been immortal, specially when they been wrapped in the benefice [advantage] of histories. (Crotch, pp. 65–66)

Higden sets the same value on history: "I pray you, who should now know emperors, wonder of the philosophers, or else follow the apostles, but [except that] their noble deeds and their wonder [wonderful] works were written in histories and so kept in mind?" (folio v, r). Indeed, the import of what Higden, Trevisa, and Caxton say about *Polychronicon* is that the worth of this—or any—book rests substantially upon its factuality and its ability to inspire right conduct. *Polychronicon* is designed to provide a record of true events, and Higden proposes to offer this factual account in a logical and comprehensible pattern. He states that he has divided *Polychronicon* into seven books to correspond to the seven days of the week of Creation and to the seven ages of the world. He begins in Book 1 with a general geography and proceeds through the remaining six books with a chronological-geographical narrative of the world from the Creation to the period of Edward III of England.

The inclusiveness of the material obscures the order, however. The text is a mixture of the many interests that prevailed in the Middle Ages, including much that now seems trivial or superstitious. *Polychronicon* offers accounts of word origins and etymologies which reflect both reverence for language and the belief that words and things are closely bound together. It catalogs inventions; it describes the curious traits of animals, including fabulous ones; it heaps together miscellaneous events in chapters which imply, by their grouping, that these assorted items bear some causal or at least symbolic relationship to one another. And indeed, *Polychronicon* shows that, to Medieval thinkers, the history of the world composes one great cosmic pattern in which human affairs and events in nature are bound together at a deep level.

Biography, sometimes with a fanciful bias, comprises a large part of the matter of the *Polychronicon*. For instance, Virgil is treated chiefly as a necromancer-philosopher rather than as a poet; he relieves Naples of a pestilence of bloodsuckers, walls his orchard with air, and builds a bridge of air;[2] and his writing of the *Aeneid* is mentioned in passing. In contrast to this account, the *Polychronicon* offers a life of Boethius which is straightforward and factual. King Arthur's story gives rise to some comments about those who have fabricated fictions about Arthur and to some misgivings about the authenticity of Arthurian stories; but after an expression of concern about the silence of French and Roman chronicles about Arthur, the chronicler concludes that every nation overpraises its own: the Greeks, Alexander; the Romans, Octavian; the English, Richard the Lionhearted; the French, Charles; and the British, Arthur.

There are fabulous stories about Lady Godiva and about the group of men and women whose dance in a churchyard causes them to be cursed by an angry priest and compelled to dance for a year. The problem of interpreting traditional stories of dubious factuality is resolved in the *Polychronicon* on the basis of the teaching function of the story. Plato and Boethius are philosophers who use feigned tales to tell truths. Aesop's fables tell one false thing by way of another, and therefore Aesop is excluded from the ranks of philosophers. On the other hand, there are long stretches of more literal record—in Book 7, Chapters 24–31, for example—which deals with the history of the Crusade under Richard the Lionhearted and treats the material factually, indeed dully.

Higden conscientiously records his sources in a manner not unlike modern documentation. He sometimes corrects them. He says that Bede errs in attributing roebuck to Ireland, but that Bede is to be excused since he had never been to Ireland and had accepted someone else's account. Higden, who remarks that his authorities do not always agree, makes repeated efforts to rationalize dubious stories. One story he neither rationalizes nor tolerates: the report that there are people on the other side of the world with their feet toward his feet; for, although the earth is round, the opposite side is all water.

Although the *Polychronicon* is universal in its range, it is British in its emphasis; for neither author, translator, nor printer felt it necessary to moderate his love of country. Book 1, Chapter 39, "De britannia," declares that Britain will be described because all this labor was begun on account of Britain. The fertility of the island is its greatest marvel, says the *Polychronicon;* it is a land of honey, milk, and cheese. It depends on no other country, but all depend upon it. Solomon would wonder at it, and Octavian desire it. Such chauvinism must have recommended the book to the printer, who was home at last after a long, if voluntary and intermittent, exile.

II   *Caxton's Revisions and Additional Book*

At the end of the seven books of the Higden-Trevisa text, Caxton explains how he has revised the first seven books to make the archaic language more readily comprehensible. He also explains his addition of the eighth book, but he sets it apart from the rest as inferior in style and as drawn only from the limited resources available to him. Since Book 8 deals with a time which in Caxton's day lay not far into the past, it provides a particular opportunity to examine the Medieval record of the historical situation in which Caxton himself lived.

Book 8 is factual and somewhat detailed, and it is also an accumulation of diverse kinds of data. For instance, the first chapter mentions a pestilence; the death of Harry, Duke of Lancaster; the marriage of Edward, Prince of Wales, to Joan of Kent; wars in France and Lombardy; John of Gaunt's receiving the title of the dead Duke of Lancaster; a great wind; the king's sons Lionel and Edmund becoming respectively the Duke of Clarence and the Earl of Cambridge;

and a royal visit by the kings of France, Cyprus, and Scotland. In a chapter of under three pages, this and more is appended to an account of the wars of France and England. A similar mixture and a similar sense of proportion can be found almost anywhere in the *Polychronicon;* for example, it records in successive sentences the deaths of Queen Jane and of the lions in the Tower of London and gives one sentence to the death of Blanche, Duchess of Lancaster.

The implication of this method of recording history is that, from one point of view, the world appeared to the Medieval chronicler as a mass of various events, all of much the same magnitude. We may also perceive here another point of view, however, in which disparate materials are understood as belonging to one pattern. For the year 1494 (the date is obviously in error), Caxton's Book 8 records three months of heavy and destructive winds in England; in France, five small stars were seen in pursuit of a large star for an hour, a voice was heard from heaven, and a copper man smote the large star with a spear and it disappeared. In other regions, the noise of armed men fighting was heard. The natural and the supernatural are here treated as intrinsically related to each other and to the events of human life.

Sometimes Book 8 supplies a bit of "local color" which would hardly be preserved except in such chronicles as this one. When Queen Isabel, the bride of Richard II, rode to her coronation, nine persons were crushed to death on London Bridge in the crowd that swarmed to see her. Sometimes the account records brutality and cruelty, as in the record of various men of rank who, at the time of the deposition of Richard II, were blinded or hanged; others were beheaded and quartered, their heads set on London Bridge, and the quarters sent to various towns. Cruelty is not confined to the affairs of the secular government. For the eleventh year of the reign of Henry IV, Book 8 records the church's persecution of the Hussites of Bohemia and the burning of heretical Lollards in Smithfield. The commendable achievements of the Council of Constance include the burning of two heretics, John Hus and Jerome of Prague.

All is not cruel, however; much is mercenary. When speaking of the exemplary King Henry V at the Battle of Agincourt, Caxton's addition notes that every Englishman in the battle came away much enriched from pillaging the French dead. Among the woes that beset England under Henry VI, not the least was the loss of a great dowry that would have come to Henry if he had carried through the negotiations designed to marry him to a daughter of the Count of Armagnac.

Higden himself supplied the key to the metaphorical pattern of the *Polychronicon:* seven books for the seven days of the Creation and the seven ages of the world. Despite Higden's clue, however, we are dazed by the multiplicity of kinds and by the sheer mass of data recorded in this history. A modern schoolchild feels the same bafflement with dates, names, places, and events in a contemporary history book, which may in fact be highly selective and focused in a clearly formulated thesis. We can hardly escape the conclusion, however, that the Middle Ages were as much aware of the multiplicity and confusion of the universe as of its unity and purpose.

III   Chronicles of England

Caxton twice printed another, smaller history book, *Chronicles of England,* in 1480 and again in 1482. Rather than being a "poly" chronicle, the *Chronicles of England* is focused on one country, but its more limited range does not enhance its factuality. *Chronicles of England,* a compendium of materials now regarded as more legend than history, begins with the story of how a king has married his thirty-three wicked daughters to thirty-three kings. His eldest daughter, Albion, leads her sisters in slitting their husbands' throats; and, as punishment, they are put to sea. On reaching land, Albion goes ashore first and names the island for herself. The sisters, who desire male company so much that the devil obliges them, bear a race of giants; and these monsters populate the island until the coming of Brute, a descendant of Aeneas of Troy, who slays the giants with the help of Corin. Cornwall is named for Corin; Britain, for Brute.

Englishmen in Caxton's day wanted to know whence they had come; they traced their ancestors into the remote and mythical past. Caxton does not tell us the names of his own parents; he records his birthplace only in a general way; but he thought highly enough of the *Chronicles,* with its account of English origins, to print the book twice. These facts reveal something about the Medieval perspective, which overlooks the immediate and the tangible and searches for the remote and the general.

Cruelty is a conspicuous aspect of the life revealed in the *Chronicles.* For example, the traitor Godwin seizes an heir apparent to the throne, Alured, son of Sweyne, and has his eyes cut out and his bowels fastened to a stake. Alured is then pricked with iron needles to make him circle the stake until he is disemboweled. The lords of

England vow to punish Godwin, who escapes to Denmark, but ultimately returns to marry his daughter to Alured's brother, St. Edward. The chronicler describes the horrors of war and famine graphically: In 1316, for instance, Barwick falls and famine is so great that people steal and eat dogs, cats, horses, and children.

Superstitious awe is also a part of the chronicler's world. He tells, for example, of King Edward's experiencing a vision in which the King of Denmark set out to invade England and drowned before arriving. The body of a man executed for his assistance to Robert the Bruce was exposed on the gallows but finally had to be removed because those set to watch it saw devils attacking and tormenting the corpse, and those who witnessed this sight either died or grew mad and ill.

As *Chronicles of England* approaches contemporary events, the details are fuller, as in the accounts of the reigns of Edward III and Henry IV. Since the accession of Henry VI occurred in the year in which Caxton was presumably born, 1422, the *Chronicles'* account of Henry's reign is of some particular interest. It includes stories of various burnings for heresy, including that of Joan of Arc; of street frays; of losses in France; of Jack Cade's rebellion; of papal schism; of the arrest of Eleanor Cobham, Duchess of Gloucester, for treason, of the accession of Edward IV in 1461. *Chronicles of England* tells us less about Caxton's particular world that we could wish, but it enables us to grasp the general tenor of the times in which he lived.

Although chronicle histories supply annals of times past, they even more importantly, perhaps, have supplied great germinal stories with which the creative imagination may work. The story of Gorboduc and his sons Ferrex and Porrex occurs in a simple half-page account in *Chronicles of England*. The story is known to the modern world through the play *The Tragedy of Gorboduc* by Thomas Norton and Thomas Sackville, which is described as "the first regular English tragedy"; but this play's tragic dimension remains more latent than realized, as in the chronicle accounts. The coming of Brute figures in many English poems, though the Brute material never becomes a great poem in its own right. *Chronicles of England* records the story of Arthur and Merlin as history; Sir Thomas Malory, Edmund Spenser, Alfred, Lord Tennyson, T. S. Eliot, and a hundred more have turned the Arthurian legend into archetypes for their own times.

The finest example, however, of the process of rendering history into art occurs with the story of King Lear. In the *Chronicles of*

England there is a simple account of Lear, who renounces his faithful daughter Cordelia for her failure to make a lavish public profession of love for him. Lear then loses his kingdom to a pair of usurping evil daughters, turns to Cordelia for aid, regains his throne, rules for three years, and is succeeded at his death by Cordelia. When Cordelia, widowed, is unable to protect herself, her evil nephews seize the throne and then fight between themselves. There is no mad Lear on the heath, no fool, no subtle probing of the tension between Lear and Cordelia, no tragic death scene. Nothing, in fact, of Shakespeare's poetry—in language, in plot rhythm, in character—is clearly foreshadowed here.

Perhaps not even Shakespeare could have moved directly from the chronicle history to the tragedy. But the accretions of folklore, the refining of plot and character, the emergence of a genre which could support a great story in isolation from the maze of distractions in the chronicle tradition, made it possible for Shakespeare to shape greatness from the ordinary.

IV   Description of Britain

In 1480 Caxton offered his readers the *Description of Britain* because an account of the land was not readily accessible and its worth was therefore insufficiently known. The book deals with factual matters such as boundaries, roads, rivers, streams, towns, and cities; with praise of Britain's fruitfulness and productivity; and with marvels such as the story of the women of the Isle of Man who sell seamen the winds bound up in the knots of a piece of thread. The little book was abridged, as Caxton's conclusion indicates, from *Polychronicon* in order to provide Englishmen with a compact and patriotic survey of their country. Deep patriotism is a trait we can attribute to Caxton on the evidence of such a volume as *Description of Britain*, but we must recognize that this little book offers something more: it provides a welcome relief from the horrors of *Polychronicon* and *Chronicles of England*; for it speaks strangely of peace, bounty, and beauty in a world racked with cruelty and suffering.

V   *Conclusion*

Caxton's chronicle histories are valuable in several ways to the study of Caxton and the Middle Ages. They provide an account of Medieval history which may not be fully reliable but to which we must turn for much of our information. They provide a background for Caxton, his world, and his time as he himself chose to perpetuate it through the printed book. And finally, they provide a paradox of which Caxton and his contemporaries were apparently only partly aware: Out of the "facts" of history grow the perceptions of art which offer truths that transcend the value of their own data. As we shall examine in some detail in Chapter 6, Caxton provided his readers with many of "the terrible feigned fables of poets [which] have much stirred and moved men to pity and conserving of justice" (Crotch, p. 65), and his prologues show that he indeed realized the value of poetry, even though his comments on history and fact seem to deny that realization.

CHAPTER 4

Caxton's Religious Texts

A S our examination of Caxton's books concerned with science, philosophy, and history has shown, nothing gave direction to Medieval life with such authority as did religious beliefs. Virtually the whole population of England was at least nominally and more often actually Christian and Roman Catholic. Yet in spite of the fact that the church exercised authority over men's ideas, their consciences, and their purses, the papal schism which began in the fourteenth century had divided both hearts and minds. Men had begun to question where the real authority of the church lay, and as a result, protests against certain elements within the Roman Catholic Church became frequent and eloquent. The fifteenth century inherited both the religious traditions and the religious unrest of the fourteenth; but with the invention of the printing press, it also acquired what was to become one of the principal instruments of the Protestant Reformation.

I *Books Used in Church Services and in Formal Devotions*

The output of Caxton's press, however, belongs entirely to the traditional and conservative side. It evidences no interest in the reformation of the hierarchical structure of the church or of its rituals and teaching; rather, it promotes their preservation and observation. Evidencing his conservatism, Caxton issued a number of religious manuals and treatises designed to get the worshipper through the church's services for an hour or a year without such serious faults and omissions as would mar the dignity, beauty, and efficacy of the service and to get him through life without such faults and omissions as would bar his terminating the earthly pilgrimage in the "Jerusalem celestial."

For example, there is a *Missale ad usum Sarum* of 1487 that Caxton did not print but commissioned; at the end appears the statement in

Latin (the language of the text) that it was printed by Guillermi (that is, William) Maynyal of Paris for "Guillermi Caxton," with Caxton's device on the verso of the last leaf. A missal is a "massbook," supplying every sung or spoken portion of the mass for the full year. The service later became virtually uniform in its prayers and other parts throughout the Roman Catholic church. In the fifteenth century, however, several "uses" other than the "Roman rite" were allowed, and the one Caxton had printed is the *Missale ad usum Sarum* (*Missal according to the use of Sarum*—Sarum is the old name for Salisbury, England).[1] The very fact that there is such a book as the missal indicates the control of the central authority of the church over the pattern and content of worship, an authority which the Reformation sought to transfer to the individual worshipper. The missal, therefore, like other books of worship printed by Caxton, bears testimony to his own conservative and nonreforming views.

Since the missal encompasses the entire year and since the service varies in part from season to season and in some points from church to church, the missal itself requires directions for its proper use. Caxton supplied these in an *Ordinale ad usum Sarum* [1479] and in Clement Maydeston's *Directorium sacerdotum* in two editions [1486] and [1488], and he also printed six editions of the *Horae ad usum Sarum*, or *Hours according to the use of Salisbury* [1477 or 1478, 1479, 1486, 1490, and two in 1491]. The "hours" are the canonical or prescribed hours of prayer, and the "book of hours" gives the proper prayers and devotions for these times. The existence of handsome manuscript books of hours with fine pictures or "illuminations" evidently moved Caxton to extend himself in the effort to provide a beautiful book of hours. The first edition of the *Sarum Hours*, known from a unique copy in the Morgan Library, contains only twelve lines to the page. Ornamented in blue, red, gold, and white, the volume is small, neat, and elegant. It constitutes the first piece of printing in England on vellum, a carefully prepared animal skin used in the Middle Ages for fine manuscript books.[2]

II Indulgences

Perhaps the most difficult of Caxton's tests for the non–Roman Catholic to comprehend are the indulgences. The indulgence procedure assumes that the church can relieve the repentant sinner of part of the temporal punishment for his sins if he has in some way merited such a special remission. Temporal punishment is any punishment limited by time, and time in the Roman Catholic view includes that spent in purgatory. In the Middle Ages, a person who contributed to a Crusade or to a similar cause might receive a written certificate of indulgence. Caxton printed a number of Latin indulgences, brief statements of what indulgence the holder would or could receive.

Indulgence might also be granted for acts of devotion. Certain blockprints, called the *Image of Pity*, show the Crucifixion in a large picture in the center and then frame it with smaller pictures that represent scenes from the life of Christ or religious symbols. Devout contemplation of the print while praying a prescribed prayer a given number of times resulted in a certain term of indulgence, according to the text accompanying the pictures. Two of the extant *Image of Pity* prints appear to have been printed by Caxton, with the verbal text in type and with the pictures in block printing. However, the amount of print offers too small a sample for bibliographers to determine with assurance whether these represent Caxton's printing.[3]

Since reformers such as John Wyclif (c. 1328–1384) gave urgent attention to abolishing the granting of indulgences, Caxton's having printed several of them offers additional evidence of his acceptance of the Roman Catholic church as he found it and of his disinclination for the reform movement.[4]

III   *Instructive Books for Persons in Holy Orders, Including Sermons*

That most fifteenth century people viewed the Roman Catholic church as rightly ordained and ordered did not prevent their feeling that it was much hindered in its execution of its mission by human frailty and perversity. Orthodox and conservative voices protested clerical and lay ignorance and error. *The Book of Divers Ghostly* [spiritual] *Matters* [1491] is a three part treatise about spiritual understanding and conduct that was designed primarily for the use of persons in religious orders who lacked learning. The first part, "Horologium sapientiae," is cast in the form of a dialogue between a disciple and Christ, Who is figured as Wisdom. The discussion focuses on the concept of God's love for man, as evidenced in the divine suffering. Part II reports the discussion of the "xii profits or advantages of tribulation" conducted by seven "masters" who had chosen tribulation as the topic most pleasing to God and profitable to their auditors. Part III contains an abstract of the Benedictine Rule for men and women of the Benedictine order who know no Latin.[5]

The emphasis of *The Book of Divers Ghostly Matters* on divine love, on the life of contemplation, on the patient endurance of tribulation, and on spiritual meekness reveals much about the Medieval mind. Life was likely to be a series of tribulations, riddled with cruelty, persecution, and humiliation. To turn in an unlovely world to the contemplation of divine love, to see tribulation as profitable, and to esteem meekness as a virtue offered consolation in the face of the hard problems of reality. The expectation that a problem can be analyzed in a sequence of parts and reduced to a pattern capable of being comprehended and therefore tolerated permeates Medieval thinking.

Caxton's religious texts include two volumes of sermons by John Mirk. Little is known of Mirk beyond the facts of his having been a "canonicus regularis" in the early fifteenth century who wrote a number of religious pieces, including these two series of sermons, one appropriate to various occasions of the year, the other explaining essential doctrines, and both designed to aid clerics in getting properly through their preaching duties.[6] Caxton printed one of them, *The Festial*, twice (1483 and [1491]), and the second, *Four Sermons*, three times [1483, 1484, and 1491]. Extracted from *The Golden Legend, The Festial* provides a short sermon on each principal feast in the year, beginning with the first Sunday in Advent. The sermons typically end with a "narracio" or story. To one of them is appended a set of "Diverse questions" which wily men may ask the unlearned priest to trap him into a display of ignorance; Mirk supplies answers.

Only a detailed study of *The Festial* could touch upon all the Medieval doctrines and preoccupations which it reveals. Perhaps most importantly, Mirk emphasizes the doctrine of *caritas*—charity—or the manifestation of love which is centered in God and which is totally unselfish because it involves a love of others for their part in God, not for their part in one's self.[7] Mirk relies on the system of typology (that is, of finding parallels between Old Testament materials and New and of treating Old Testament figures as types or partial revelations of Christ, Who is fully revealed in the New Testament). The famous New Testament story of Mary and Martha provides Mirk with an allegory. He interprets Martha, the sister who is busy with household chores, as representative of the active life or the life of holy service in active pursuits; and he presents Mary as representative of the contemplative life or the life of withdrawal from active service into the spiritual exercise of the contemplation of God.

He explores various relations between biblical materials and church doctrine, often using numbers as a key to the analogy. The biblical story of the five loaves and two fishes is explained as using the five loaves to represent contrition, confession, satisfaction, fear of relapse into sin, and perseverance; the fish represent prayers and alms.[8]

In *Four Sermons*, which directs each sermon to an important topic, the first one explains certain doctrinal matters which are essential for man's salvation: the Lord's Prayer; the Apostles' Creed; the Ten Commandments; the Seven Sacraments as taught by the Roman Catholic church (Baptism, Confirmation, Shrift or Confession, Housel or Holy Communion, Anointing or Extreme Unction, Priesthood, and Marriage); and the Seven Deeds of Mercy (feeding the hungry, giving water to the thirsty, giving clothing, giving shelter, visiting the sick, liberating prisoners, and burying the poor when they are dead); the Seven Ghostly or Spiritual Deeds of Mercy (teaching the unlearned, counseling him who asks, chastising sinners, comforting the sorrowing, forgiving trespassers, suffering trespass meekly, and praying for enemies and for sinners); the seven principal Virtues (Faith; Hope or the expectation of being saved by God's mercy; Charity; "Rightwiseness" or paying what is due, as in being thankful to God for good gifts; Wisdom or knowing good from evil; Strength against adversity and prosperity; and Measure, or striking a balance between too much and too little); and the Seven Deadly Sins (Pride, Envy, Wrath, Covetousness, Gluttony, Sloth, and Lechery). Mirk describes the nine pains of hell and the seven bodily and the seven spiritual joys of heaven. This first sermon in *Four Sermons* is very full of doctrine and very long. The second of the four sermons explains penance; the third, excommunication; and the fourth, the prayers which should be offered on Sunday and for whom.

Both *The Festial* and *Four Sermons* provide an excellent introduction to the content, the emphasis, and the method of Medieval exegesis and preaching. They also endeavor to reduce the complex and abstract to sets of concrete, countable, easily learned patterns—a characteristic found in many of the books Caxton printed, whether religious or secular. Indeed, the repeated editions of *The Festial* and *Four Sermons* indicate the enthusiasm of Caxton and his public for them.

Caxton's zeal for such material is also indicated by the fact that he both translated from the French and printed the *Doctrinal of Sapience* [1489], ascribing the original to Guy de Roye through some error, for this work is now regarded as anonymous.[9] The *Doctrinal,* like *The Festial* and *Four Sermons,* is directed toward supplying priests with a guide to what they should "learn and teach" their people. The *Doctrinal* contains ninety-three chapters; and, although orderly presentation is not the author's strong point, he manages to survey various topics considered necessary to the understanding of essential doctrine. While the *Doctrinal of Sapience* is not always lively in style, its soberness is well intended, and the author uses illustrations and examples to make the abstract and abstruse clear.

IV   *Books of Religious Instruction for Laymen*

Much the same religious instruction that was published by Caxton for members of the clergy and of the religious orders can also be found in the books he published for use by laymen. *The Royal Book* [1487], for example, indicates in both the Prologue and the Epilogue that Caxton means it to be read by all; for, though it is called "a book for a king," "the Holy Scripture calls every man a king . . ." (Crotch, p. 102). The text discusses the Ten Commandments, the Apostles' Creed, the Seven Deadly Sins, the Lord's Prayer, the seven gifts of the Holy Ghost, the active and contemplative lives, and the necessity for expecting and preparing for death. Topics are illustrated throughout with images and examples which show how much Medieval theology relied on the visual and tactile to make its abstractions comprehensible.

Another book of religious instruction for laymen is *The Book of Good Manners* (1487). In the Prologue to *The Book of Good Manners* Caxton relates that the recently deceased William Praat, a mercer, had given him a French book on manners. Since man is distinguished from the beasts by manners, "for manners make man," and since the book rests on substantial authority, Caxton obeyed his friend's request that he "instantly" translate it for the use of English readers (Crotch, pp. 99, 100). Although the book is called *The Book of Good Manners,* it is concerned with "manners" defined as "moral conduct," not with etiquette. Book I treats the Seven Deadly Sins and their opposite Virtues as the foundation for all that is to come. Book II treats the good manners of churchmen; Book III, of princes and the aristocracy; Book IV, of the common man seen in various capacities; Book V, death and doomsday. *The Book of Good Manners* makes a division of the world into three estates—church, nobility, and commons—and into other groups such as young and old, married and single, and so on. Although common good sense generally prevails, some of the stories which illustrate erroneous ways of acting are sensational and designed to alarm.

V Death as a Focus for Man's Thought

As these various texts show, Medieval churchmen regarded the knowledge of certain doctrines as essential to both priest and layman in order to prepare for death and eternity.[10] Caxton printed several books which deal with death as a chief topic: *The Cordial* (1479), *The Art and Craft to Know Well to Die* [1490]. *The Craft for to Die for the Health of a Man's Soul (Ars moriendi)* [1491], *Deathbed Prayers* [1487?/1485?], and *The Pilgrimage of the Soul* (1483).

Caxton printed the translation of *The Cordial* made by Earl Rivers; he may also have been responsible for the printing of the French text in Bruges [1476]. One version of the French title, *Les quatre choses derrenieres (The Four Last Things)*, states the focus of the book: on death, doomsday, hell, and heaven. *The Cordial* urges that the certainty of death for the body should cause man to despise worldly vanity and do penance.

The Art and Craft to Know Well to Die and *The Craft for to Die for the Health of a Man's Soul* are two versions of the same general tract, but the first is approximately double the length of the second. Both are manuals for the priest or layman who must guide another's deathbed thoughts. The single leaf *Deathbed Prayers* contains a series of petitions suited to the dying.[11]

The Pilgrimage of the Soul, an anonymous translation from a French poem, Deguilleville's *Le Pèlerinage de l'âme*, formerly attributed to John Lydgate, is a dream allegory of the long journey to the heavenly Jerusalem, a journey which can only be completed when death has parted body and soul.[12] *The Pilgrimage of the Soul* differs from Caxton's other treatises about the contemplation of death because it conveys its message through a narrative rather than through direct exposition of its topic. (The most casual reader will be aware of the general resemblances of plot and theme to John Bunyan's *Pilgrim's Progress.*) Perhaps for the very reason that it chooses to instruct by entertaining, *The Pilgrimage of the Soul* illustrates how seriously Medieval man took the injunction to consider death.

VI   *Three Volumes of Religious Biography*

One of the most arduous and financially burdensome of Caxton's undertakings was the translation and printing of *The Golden Legend* in two editions [1484 and 1487].[13] *The Golden Legend,* a vast collection of saints' lives originally compiled in Latin by Jacobus de Varagine, is directed to the hope that readers will grow more virtuous through the study of the examples provided by holy persons. Caxton's Epilogue explains that the title of the book is *Legenda aurea* or *The Golden Legend* because just as gold surpasses other metals, this book surpasses other books; but Caxton's most personal comment is probably his remark in the Prologue about being rendered "half desperate" (Crotch, p. 70) by the size of the thing, a feeling with which his readers may sympathize.

In contrast to the lengthy *Golden Legend, The Life of Saint Winifred* [1487?, 1485?] is a small volume that contains an isolated Welsh saint's life and a Latin service for her. Besides these works, *Vitas patrum,* or *Lives of the Fathers,* was, according to de Worde, translated by Caxton and finished on the day of his death in 1491. This work contains a long account of the fathers who lived lives of penance in the desert, but an occasional account concerns a woman saint or sinner. De Worde printed Caxton's translation in 1495.

VI   *The Bible*

A conspicuous omission among Caxton's religious texts is the Bible, an omission for which the Roman Catholic church's attitude toward translations of the Bible, expressed in the Oxford "Constitutions" of 1408 in the wake of John Wyclif's vernacular translation, is generally adduced as an explanation. Caxton printed the *Psalter* [1483] in Latin but not an entire Latin Bible. Despite the fact that the basic aims of Caxton's press were to provide English books for English readers and to make these edifying and instructive, Caxton may have bowed to the church's dictum that the English Bible provided too great an opportunity for unlearned men to render unlicensed interpretations.

It has been claimed, however, that Caxton did in effect print the first English Bible, though an incomplete one, by including most of the Pentateuch and the Gospels in *The Golden Legend.* Moreover, one other piece of evidence implies that Caxton did not disapprove the translation of the Bible into English; for in the Proem to the

Polychronicon, he states that John Trevisa translated the Bible. That Trevisa did in fact translate the Bible is not certainly proved, but the inclusion of a translation of the Bible among the commendable works of Trevisa implies Caxton's approval of the act of translating it.[14]

In summary, scholarly speculation suggests that Caxton may have meant to print a Bible but somehow failed to get it done, perhaps through hesitation, age, or the pressure of other tasks. The evidence for this supposition lies only in the fact that most of nine books of the Bible do appear in Caxton's translation of *The Golden Legend*, in the hint that he approved of the Bible's being translated, and in the fact that he printed a large body of religious books. Weighing against the possibility is the fact that, while Caxton showed courage in some of his publications, to stand against the church would have been an act of quite another kind of daring from hazarding a reprimand from Richard III or the Duke of Clarence.

Tradition, not daring, is the key to Caxton's religious pieces. They reveal what the Roman Catholic church long had taught and was teaching and practicing in the fifteenth century. They bear evidence that Caxton's religion was sincere and informed but was in keeping with fifteenth century orthodoxy. When he invited men to reform, the invitation was for the reform of themselves, not of the church. His religious books emphasize not so much ways to think about the church and its doctrines as ways to act in response to the church's established doctrines.

CHAPTER 5

Caxton's Books Concerned with the Secular Order

I *Theoretical and Practical Examinations of the Patterns of the World*

IN dealing with temporal reality, Medieval writers sought formulations which would express the infinitely varied and constantly shifting facts of the social and political world in comprehensible patterns. The concept of the Great Chain of Being pictures all of creation ranged in an orderly progression in which the angels, then men, and then the lower animals are each fixed in a place, are forbidden to move up or down in the Chain, but are endowed with an attribute of strength which makes survival possible. Extended to the social and political orders, the way of thinking that produced the concept of the Great Chain implies that every rank and office carries privileges and responsibilities within a rigidly stratified system.

Another way of explaining the social order is found in the ninth century formula of King Alfred, in which society is said to consist of three ranks or estates: those who pray, those who fight, and those who plow. Such stratification had never worked absolutely, as everyone knew if he thought about it; it was, for instance, well known that William the Conqueror had a burgher as a grandfather; and although Alfred's triparite division continued to operate in men's minds, the merchant class had emerged as a distinct group, as Caxton's life illustrates. By the fifteenth century, social and political mobility and even a degree of democracy were evident.[1]

The chessboard, with its rigidly drawn squares and its pieces moving according to rules, but nonetheless moving, is an apt symbol of the love of order and of the recognition of change which the fifteenth century displays. Jacobus de Cessolis's Latin *The Game and Play of the Chess*, which Caxton translated from a

French translation made by Jean Ferron and Jean de Vignay and first printed at Bruges [1475], second edition [Westminster, 1482], reveals a dual adherence to rigidity and systemization and to progress and alteration. It offers instruction in right conduct for all orders of life within a social and political hierarchy that ranges from the king downwards. *The Game and Play of the Chess* assumes that the hierarchy is right but that those who hold places in it may be wrong.

Kings, queens, and judges represent an established authority. Because of their position, they carry the responsibility to provide justice and order. If they do not fulfill their duties, violent measures may be taken to correct them. Even so, the expectation of justice seems not to have been high. Tyberius, when asked why he left men in office so long, is said to have related the story of someone's driving flies off a sick man, who complained that, to his greater pain, well-fed flies would be replaced by hungry ones. Officers who had already won riches did less injury than poor new ones.[2]

The Game and Play of the Chess recognizes that changes in the hierarchy are possible. If the pawns, which represent the commons, cross the entire board uncaptured, they acquire the queen's privileges. The author takes some care to insist that the upper classes ought not to despise the commons, for many commoners have risen to high places—David, a shepherd, became a king—and nobles may be brought low. The social point of view is ambivalent when it suggests that persons in low estate should be respected because they might rise, but there is recognition of the possibility of change.

Some of the advice in *The Game and Play of the Chess* must have profited commercially oriented fifteenth century London little. It contains, for example, the story of a knight who declared that money should be no more regarded than dung and who prohibited trade except by barter. But, because of the political upheavals of the times, this same knight's decree that the people should be obedient servants to the prince and that the prince should be a protector of the people and a prosecutor of wrongdoers surely struck a responsive chord. W. J. Blyth Crotch[3] indicates, moreover, that the lament for the decay of the country, the prayer for the king, and the complaints against dishonest and self-seeking advocates are Caxton's additions to *The Game and Play of the Chess*. These aspects of the work, which must have come from the printer's heart, must have spoken to the hearts of readers, as they may even yet do. *The Game and Play of the Chess* is about no other game than that of life. With its readability, its homely wisdom, and its realism, it is little inferior to Sir Thomas Hoby's famous translation of *The Book of the Courtier*.[4]

Unlike *The Game and Play of the Chess*, *The Order of Chivalry* [1484], is, as its title indicates, directed only to the aristocratic level of society. The book's Prologue, itself translated from the French, states that, just as God rules the seven planets and other parts of the universe, great rulers rule the knights, and the knights rule the commons. Having offered this rationale for the existing social order, the text then describes how a young squire who is on his way to receive knighthood comes upon a knight, now old and turned hermit, from whom he inquires about the duties of knighthood. The relationship of chivalry to sanctity is made explicit by the presence of the hermit-knight as teacher, but also notable is the fact that chivalry, essentially based on action, can be recorded and learned from books. The hermit declares that there must be books on chivalry; great wrong is done the science of chivalry when it is not recorded in books and studied. After the squire is given a book on chivalry and told to study and teach others, the old hermit-knight insists that, just as clerks have schools, so should knights have schools taught by themselves; for a tailor would not go to a carpenter to learn to sew.

The Order of Chivalry provides an explanation of the origin of chivalry: When virtue was lost in the world and trouble came in its stead, people divided themselves into groups and chose leaders known for their loyalty, strength, and courage to protect them. The political structure is, therefore, a humanly devised and not a divinely ordered scheme and is, furthermore, a substitute for a natural order. Men rather than women serve as knights, because the male is superior to the female in wit, understanding, and strength; but he is more inclined to viciousness.

The Order of Chivalry teaches that the knight's first duty is a defense of the faith and then of the land. He must protect women and children and the old and the weak. He must defend the roads, the land, and the laborers. He must not destroy land, cattle, and buildings or commit robbery; rather, he must seek to punish those who do wicked deeds. He should have a castle, a horse, towns, and cities suitable to the exercise of these duties; he must rule himself as well as the land; he must exercise his body in jousts, tourneys, and hunts; and his soul must develop all the virtues.

Since the responsibilities of the knight are heavy, the process of examining a squire who wishes knighthood should be a serious matter. He should be questioned by a knight as to whether he loves and fears God, and then examined as to his courage and virtue. The knight is required to know the Seven Virtues, which are the way to good customs and to heavenly glory: the theological virtues of Faith, Hope, and Charity; the cardinal virtues of Justice, Prudence, Strength, and Temperance. How these stand in opposition to the Seven Deadly Sins is illustrated by various examples. The knight's equipment is analyzed in terms of symbolic values. The fact that his horse's head precedes its body is said to show that reason should lead the knight.

If the candidate for knighthood proves fit, he undergoes a ritual involving confession, communion, fasting, prayer, and a night's watch; and he is then received into the order of chivalry on a date that is preferably of religious significance. He should hear mass, swear before the altar to sustain his role, and hear a sermon on the Apostles' Creed, the Ten Commandments, and the Sacraments. Both the religious instruction and the practices necessary for the knight are the same as those emphasized in Caxton's overtly religious texts.

In some respects, *The Order of Chivalry* is a manual born out of its time. It was printed in the hope of restoring and preserving chivalry in a period in which it could succeed in preserving only a record of chivalric ideals which were never attained or attainable and which were certainly not a realistic goal of late fifteenth century military life. Although the book is, therefore, an example of Caxton's ties with a dying past, *The Order of Chivalry* was not merely a book of remote memories for Caxton and his readers. About a century later, Spenser's *Faerie Queene* portrayed the perfect gentleman and knight, and Sir Philip Sidney became one of the most admired men of his time because of his knightly valor and grace; the chivalric ideal long retained its vitality as a concept if not as a practice.[5]

But if *The Order of Chivalry* is theoretical and idealistic, Chistine de Pisan's *Feats of Arms*, published in 1489 in Caxton's translation, is practical and realistic. Although written by a woman, a widow who was engaged in supporting herself and her family by writing, *Feats of Arms* must have been regarded by Caxton and by Henry VII, who asked that Caxton publish it, as a practical manual of arms and battle.[6] Idealism has little place in it, for this work tells how to cope with traitors and thieves, how to trap the enemy into ambush or starve him into submission, and how to encourage men to unusual valor.

Christine presents, however, a conservative view of courage. She cites Scipio Africanus as having said that his mother raised him to be an emperor, not a fighter, and Gaius Maximus as having refused a challenge to single combat by saying that, if he had found his life noxious, he could have found a way to end it. Charles V of France gives her a nobler note on which to end these examples; for having been reproved for making money payments instead of fighting to recover some fortresses, Charles replies that what can be bought with money ought not to be bought with human blood.

Christine advocates devious methods in combat, but she rebukes the inclination to fight in an unjust cause. Even the common soldier is obliged to ask about the morality of the cause and not merely about the wages. She also explores theoretical questions which bear on moral judgments: May a prisoner of war escape? May an emperor fight against a Pope? If a man holds lands under both of two opposing factions, which must he serve? May mercenaries be employed?

Whatever skill a man has or however right his cause or conduct, whatever his prospects seem to be at the outset, war is risky, Christine warns, and may turn out disastrously. She explains how to fight, but she advises against it. Little in this practical, clear-sighted manual calls up visions of knights in shining armor rushing to the rescue of damsels in distress. It emphasizes the problems of food, money, deserters, traitors, spies, cowards, defeat. There can be no doubt that the mercer-turned-printer who printed for the kings of England in one of the nation's beleaguered times was a man who knew the practicalities of his world. The printing of Christine's book indicates Caxton's and Henry VII's realistic view of warfare.

The issuance of books with two such different views of chivalry as *The Order of Chivalry* and *Feats of Arms* from the same press within a period of five years demonstrates that theory and practice might be radically at odds. Similarly, the king's court can be regarded in one text as designed to provide order while it is roundly criticized in another. *The Curial* [1483] is described by Caxton as a letter from Alain Chartier advising his brother against coming to court by detailing its wretchedness. Chartier defines the court as an assembly of persons met for the purpose of betraying one another. He calls life at court "a poor riches, an abundance miserable, a highness that falleth, an estate not stable, a certainty trembling, and an evil life."[1] That Caxton printed *The Curial* suggests that he did not so wholly reverence the aristocracy as to feel that it could not be improved.

II *Instructional Books for Boys and Young Women*

We have looked, in Chapter 1, at an instructional book for young boys, *The Book of Courtesy*. Another little book for children, John Lydgate's *Stans puer ad mensam* (1477 or 1478), is in verse, and it begins:

> My dear child first thyself enable
> With all thine heart to virtuous discipline.
> Afore thy sovereign standing at the table.
> Dispose thy youth after my doctrine.
> To all nurture thy corage [heart] incline.[8]

The young reader is given such advice as "Keep foot and finger still in peace" (l. 7).

Women figure less largely than men in Caxton's work, but he published in 1484 the lengthy advice of Geoffroy de la Tour Landry to his motherless daughters, *The Book of the Knight of the Tower*.[9] With that dual emphasis which regularly appears in such pieces in the Middle Ages, both Caxton in the Prologue and the knight in the text express the hope that the book will be useful in mortal life and will direct its readers to immortality. There are numerous examples of women who behave ill by turning their heads too easily, like a tortoise or a weathervane; by taking up new fashions in clothes too rapidly; and by entering vainly into disputes with men, which they must lose because men are better able to conduct an argument. The serious discussion of good and evil women begins with Eve, who receives nine chapters, one for each of her follies. Lot's wife; one of the daughters of Jacob; Tamar; the "queen" who tried to seduce Joseph; the daughters of Moab; and others are introduced as examples to show that the wearing of new-fangled clothes displeased God and caused the Great Deluge.

The whole text illustrates precept by example—another evidence of the preference of Caxton and his era for books that teach through stories. One illustration of particular interest accompanies the injunction to women not to tell others about their husbands' secrets. A squire binds his wife to secrecy, and as a test of her obedience, he tells her he has laid two eggs. She cannot keep such a piece of news to herself, and as the story is retold, the two eggs become five. When the squire confronts the wife with his knowledge of her breach of secrecy, she feels herself to be a fool.[10] If she thinks her husband a fool too, the story does not say so.

The Knight of the Tower contains a long account of an argument between the knight-author and his now dead wife in which he makes the case for a secret, sensuous, illicit love affair between persons not married to each other—the system called by modern scholars, for want of a better name, "courtly love." The wife's reply, supporting fidelity in marriage, is presented as bettering the husband's argument. [11] The knight finally ends his discourse by telling his daughters that a word out of the mouth is like a shaft out of a bow: it will not stop until it hits something. Caxton's colophon is short; perhaps the knight has left little to be said.

III Books of Vocabulary, Grammar, and Rhetoric

Caxton, an ex-mercer, provided one book that was specifically designed for merchants, a French-English word and phrase list that is known by various titles: *Instructions for Travellers; Vocabulary in French and English; Dialogues in French and English;* or *Doctrine to learn French and English* [1480]. The book, as its titles indicate, was designed for those who traveled and traded abroad. It begins with a "Table" setting forth the order of the material: names of the Trinity; greetings between men; household articles; names of beasts, birds, fish, meat, fruits, trees, soups, drinks, cloth, towns, fairs, hides, skins; and, among other items, a long list of different tradesmen.

The dialogues in *Vocabulary in French and English* sometimes take an odd turn; for example, the maid who is being sent to market replies to her master's list of edible meats with a list of inedible ones, including apes and elephants. The book is valued among modern scholars, however, for what it tells the historian about Medieval crafts and trades as well as for its philological interests. It enables us to see not only men in the marketplace who are dealing with millers, scriveners, money-changers, and dishonest merchants, but also the family at home, endeavoring to live in peace, but beating the children if necessary, if the advice in the *Vocabulary* was followed. Whether *Vocabulary in French and English* was translated by Caxton or by someone else is disputed, but we know that he printed it with the design of assisting travelers in foreign parts. Today, this work assists us in learning about middle class life of the Middle Ages and in witnessing small details with unexpected intimacy. [12]

The *Vocabulary* teaches French and English. Latin, however, remained the language of the learned, and the incipient scholar and the rhetorician are provided for by Caxton, though not magnificently, in *Donatus* or *Donatus melior* [1487], a famous grammar, and in L. G. Traversagni's *Nova rhetorica* [1479] and an abridgement of *Nova rhetorica, Epitoma sive isagogicum margarite castigate eloquentie* [1480].[13]

IV   A *Medical Treatise*

Caxton printed a solitary medical treatise, *Governal of Health; Medicina stomachi* [1491], a small book of less than fifty pages. In a day when medicine was compounded from all manner of impalatables and administered by the signs of the zodiac,[14] the *Governal* is remarkable for its brevity, practicality, and common sense. If it recommends some practices that are not likely to assist greatly, it avoids those likely to be harmful and is a thoroughly readable little book. In general, it makes eight suggestions for health: be discreet in eating; exercise enough to produce sweat and quicken breathing; chew food well; eat when hungry; sleep until wakened naturally; eat when happy; avoid cold in winter and bloodletting in summer; and season food with saffron, which aids the digestion, retards aging, and produces contentment.

Upon arising in the morning, a man should put on fresh clothes if he possesses any, walk about a little, and comb his hair to draw out the vapors which have risen from the stomach. Great prelates, whose dignity will not allow their exercising in public, are advised to have some means of doing so in their chambers. A great deal of advice focuses on the necessity for choosing a diet suited to the temperament—a choleric man can eat strong foods, for instance, but delicate foods will be corrupted by the heat of his stomach. After eating, one should sleep on the right side, so that the liver is under the stomach, like fire under a pot. The concluding division of the book is in rime and is chiefly a counsel to moderation; the reader is advised to avoid bad wine and raw meat and to keep his head well wrapped from the cold.

Even with his enthusiasm for history, Caxton could hardly have guessed how much later ages have cherished the record of some of the things which he knew about life and labor in the fifteenth century. Some of the practical advice that Caxton might have provided—how to conduct the wool trade, how to print and market books—is lacking. Certain general concepts of the time, however, are available to us through those of Caxton's books that we have surveyed in this chapter. These books provide a necessary corrective to the impression of the moral and religious treatises; for, although Medieval man was endlessly enjoined to think of death, he also thought of fighting, of getting ahead, of marriage, of food and drink, and of health.

CHAPTER 6

Caxton's Prose and Verse Narratives

THE Medieval mind, as it is reflected in the books from Caxton's press which we have examined, sought wholeness but experienced multeity. It sought truth through fact, it often denied the value of the nonfactual; it nevertheless cherished the nonfactual, and it frequently and ironically mistook fiction for fact. It paid homage to edification and instruction, but it often engaged in merely entertaining itself. William Caxton apparently shared in these paradoxical views. As a culminating, ultimate, and certainly unintended paradox, he made his most significant contribution as translator, editor, publisher, and critic through the fictional narratives in prose and verse that he presented to his public. More than a third of the total number of titles printed by Caxton are fictional narratives, and a very high proportion of the works published by him which continue to hold reader interest are narratives. Caxton himself recognized the value of the fictional narrative, as his prologues and epilogues testify, though this recognition may, in fact, have been more intuitive than conscious.

What the fictional narrative at its best can accomplish is the creation of a reality which at once transcends the contradictions and imperfections of temporal reality and reduces time and space to a patterned and measurable whole. It enables the human mind to grasp and understand its own particular relationship to the universe— exactly the value which the Middle Ages sought in nonfiction. Fiction can provide an avenue into human personality and into the full dimensions of life which direct experience does not always provide. Fiction can approach a truth about the human condition which subsumes partial truths. The prose and verse narratives published by Caxton, many of them translated by him, sometimes do and sometimes, perhaps more often, do not achieve this kind of perception. Caxton's inferior narratives, however, are instructive through their shortcomings, for rough or imperfect narratives may enable us to examine the craftsman's work before the ultimate finish of perfection produces the art which conceals its artistry under the cover of inspiration.

I   *Classical Stories*

The first of Caxton's prose narratives is also his first independently printed book. Its very name, *The Recuyell*, or collection, *of the Historyes of Troye* [1475], is a warning that the book contains a mixed genre, part history and part fiction, and that the plot will be long and winding. It has, however, a basic structure in being developed around three destructions of Troy. The author-compiler of the French text which Caxton translated, Raoul Lefèvre, sees an additional structural pattern in the fact that each book has a chief hero—Perseus, Hercules, or Hector. Book I, centered, more or less, in Perseus and his marriage, contains only a small proportion of Trojan episodes, but it ends with Hercules's destruction of the city's walls: The Trojans had refused to pay the gods for building the walls, and they lost their city as a result.

Book II contains a second destruction of Troy, this time in vengeance for the inhospitality shown the questers after the Golden Fleece; but the hero, Hercules, having destroyed the city a second time, goes to his own death and destruction. Book III relates the rebuilding of Troy and then its third destruction after Priam's son carries off Helen, the story made famous by the *Iliad*. The formal elements of a balanced plot are present in the large outlines of the story, but they are so heavily overladen with detail that the structure is obscured. Although *The Recuyell* attempts to record life, both author and translator lacked the gift of selectivity which would have enabled them to keep the significance of the material in focus.

The Recuyell is treated in this discussion as a fictional narrative, but Lefèvre and Caxton might have classified it among historical accounts. Although Lefèvre cites his sources and clearly considers them to be authoritative, Caxton is aware that all the sources do not agree. He warns his reader that Dictes, Dares, and Homer tell different versions of the story and that the names of the characters are given in various forms, but, says Caxton in his Epilogue,

all accord in conclusion, the general destruction of that noble city of Troy and the death of so many noble princes, as kings, dukes, earls, barons, knights, and common people, and the ruin irreparable of that city, that never since was re-edified, which may be example to all men during the world how dreadful and jeopardus it is to begin a war, and what harms, losses, and death followeth. Therefore th'apostle saith "All that is written is written to our doctrine," which doctrine for the common weal I beseech God may be taken in such place and time as shall be most needful in increasing peace, love, and charity, which grant us He that suffered for the same to be crucified on the rood tree. And say we all Amen for charity. (Crotch, p. 8)

Raoul Lefèvre furnished Caxton with a second narrative, *The History of Jason* [1477], in which the plot is put together in the simple fashion that is sometimes called the "clothesline technique" because one episode after another is attached, like clothes hung on a washline, to the plot line and the time sequence involves simple chronological time. Although Lefèvre demonstrates more selectivity in the choice of his materials in *Jason* than he did in *The Recuyell of the Historyes of Troye*, the characters are not developed with much insight, and no significant theme focuses the episodes. The material is capable of an archetypal rendering which would give it psychological significance, but it receives no such development here. Perhaps the link to Troy, the fictive original home of the Britons, together with the romantic and gory fascinations of the plot, led Caxton to translate and print *Jason*.

Most unfortunately, the Classical world also yielded Caxton another book, *Eneydos*. Caxton used a French prose text derived from the *Aeneid* as the basis for his own translation, and his Prologue offers an account of how he selected his text:

After diverse works made, translated, and achieved, having no work in hand, I sitting in my study where as lay many diverse pamphlets and books, [it] happened that to my hand came a little book in French which late was translated out of Latin by some noble clerk of France, which book is named *Eneydos*, made in Latin by that noble poet & great clerk Virgil, which book I saw over and read therein. . . . In which book I had great pleasure by cause of the fair and honest terms & words in French. Which I never saw to fore [before] like, nor none so pleasant nor so well ordered, which book as me seemed [it seemed to me] should be much requisite to noble men to see as well for the eloquence as the histories. (Crotch, p. 107)

Caxton admired his French book, but it is a poor representation of the *Aeneid*. The plot has been reorganized along chronological lines, its proportions have been altered, and the style of Caxton's translation, with its incessant synonyms, does nothing to speed the tedious

narrative. In fact, one of Caxton's earliest critics has remained his
most virulent and eloquent. Gavin Douglas, a Scots poet (1474?–
1522), is as famous for his wrath with Caxton as for his own translation
of the *Aeneid*. Douglas begins his Prologue with praise of Virgil:

> Laud, honor, praisings, thanks infinite
> To thee and thy sweet, ornate, fresh writing,
> Most reverend Virgil, of Latin poets prince,
> Gem of ingenuity and flood of eloquence,
> Thou peerless pearl, patron of poetry . . . .[1]

Douglas says of Caxton:

> William Caxton, of the English nation,
> In prose has printed a book of English gross,
> Calling it Virgil's *Aeneid*,
> Which that he says from French he did translate,
> It has nothing to do therewith, God knows;
> They are no more alike than the devil and Saint Augustine.[2]

Douglas has a good deal more to say in the way of the particulars of
Caxton's transgressions, for the Scots poet exclaims, "I spitted for
despite [contempt] to see so spoilt" Virgil's "ornate, golden verses."[3]
   A close comparison between Virgil's *Aeneid* and Caxton's translation is impossible for the reason that Caxton is not close to Virgil.
What has happened to the Latin epic can be glimpsed, however, by
looking at Caxton's opening in comparison to Virgil's. Caxton begins:

For to hear, open, and declare the matter of which hereafter shall be made
mention, it behoveth to presuppose that Troy, the great capital city and the
excellentest of all the cities of the country & region of Asia, was constructed
and edified by the right puissant & renowned king Priamus, son of
Laomedon, descended of th'ancient stock of Dardanus by many degrees,
which was son of Jupiter & of Electra his wife, after [according to] the fictions
poetic, and the first original beginning of the genealogy of kings. And the said
Troy was environed [surrounded] in form of seige and of excidion [destruc-
tion; this occurrence in Caxton is the only example of "excidion" in English
cited in *The Oxford English Dictionary*], by Agamemnon, king in Greece,
brother of Menelaus which was husband to Helen. The which Agamemnon,
assembled and accompanied with many kings, dukes, earls, and great
quantity of other princes & Greeks innumerable, had the magistration
[command; again, this occurrence is the only example cited in *The Oxford
English Dictionary* of "magistration" in English] and universal goverance of
all th' excersite [exercise, drill] and host to-fore [before] Troy.[4]

Virgil begins in quite another way:

> Arma virumque cano, Troiae qui primus ab oris
> Italiam fato profugus Laviniaque venit
> litora, multum ille et terris iactatus et alto
> vi superum, saevae memorem Iunonis ob iram,
> multa quoque et bello passus, dum conderet urbem
> inferretque deos Latio; genus unde Latinum
> Albanique patres atque altae moenia Romae.[5]

Douglas's translation does not correspond line for line with Virgil, but it is quite close:

> The battles and the man I will describe
> From Troy's bounds first that, fugitive,
> By fate to Italy came and the coast of Lavinia.
> O'er land and sea driven with great pain
> By force [power] of [the] gods above, from every stead [place],
> Of [by] cruel Juno through [because of] old remembered wrath.
> Great pain in battle suffered he also
> Before he his gods brought into Latium
> And built the city from which, of noble fame,
> The Latin people taken have their name,
> And also the fathers, princes of Alba,
> Came, and the wall-builders of great Rome also.[6]

The pedestrian quality of Caxton's text and its great distance from Virgil are apparent from these samples. As Douglas exclaims, "He runs so far from Virgil in many place,/In so prolix and tedious fashion."[7]

The matter of Rome served Caxton somewhat poorly. But at the least he recognized the value of the Trojan and Roman stories. He admired language. He was diligent as a translator, making available to English readers what no other translator had done. He is not the last translator who has failed to do justice to Virgil. Caxton's *Eneydos* cannot be admired; but perhaps Gavin Douglas grew more wroth with the printer than was deserved.

II   *Fables*

Higden's *Polychronicon*, in its zeal to advocate historical truth, condemns works which tell one feigned thing by way of another. Caxton, however, not only modernized, extended, and printed

Higden's *Polychronicon;* he also translated the *Fables of Aesop* (specifically drummed out of the corps of philosphers by *Polychronicon*), *The Metamorphoses of Ovid,* and the anonymous *Reynard the Fox.* The *Fables of Aesop* as Caxton translated and printed it (1484) begins with the life of Aesop, who was born deformed and speechless but who was granted speech and wisdom because of an act of hospitality. Aesop, who was sold into slavery by a jealous and wicked steward, served his masters well and wittily, but he was finally unjustly executed. The true Aesopian fables are chiefly concerned with animals —"The Cock and the Precious Stone," "The Fox and the Grapes," "The Dog in the Manger"—but the Caxton collection also includes "The Fables of Avyan," "The Fables of Alfonce," and "The Fables of Poge the Florentyn." In these various additions the characters are often human; in "Poge the Florentyn" they are monsters—a two-headed cat, a two-headed calf, a cow which gives birth to a serpent, and the like—quite enough to rouse Higden's displeasure. Scholars credit to Caxton's own composition two brief, untitled stories which conclude the *Aesop* collection. The first, which begins "There was in a certain town a widower wooed a widow . . . ," twists the Medieval injunction to scorn temporal life and seek eternity into a justification for rushing headlong into death through the pursuit of sensual pleasure. The second, embedded in Caxton's Epilogue, begins "Now then I will finish all these fables with this tale that followeth . . . that there were dwelling in Oxford two priests . . . ." In the tale, a poor priest shows his old friend who has become a rich dean that the true measure of success in life is the attainment of heavenly reward.[8]

The Metamorphoses of Ovid, translated by Caxton in 1480 but apparently never printed by him, is concerned with the transformations—metamorphoses—by which persons in some dire strait are turned into various animals, plants, or trees. In a not altogether logical way, these transformations are explained as reflections of the many changes to which the world is subject: Seasons change; skeletons of sea creatures are found where there is now only dry land; water may be sometimes fresh and sometimes salt. Since the French translator had greatly expanded the fragments of the Troy story found in Ovid, *The Metamorphoses* as Caxton translated it has become another Troy book.[9]

Ovid relates not only to Troy but to another matter close to Caxton's heart: Geoffrey Chaucer. One of the changes on which the French Ovid comments is the fact that fame alters and distorts the records of what a man has done, and to this statement Caxton adds the observation that Chaucer demonstrates this fact in his *Book of Fame*.[10] *The Metamorphoses of Ovid* was frequently a source book for Chaucer. Indeed, it almost appears that Caxton chose his books for their connection with Chaucer—Cicero, Cato, *Reynard,* Ovid, Virgil, Gower, Lydgate, and all the Troy material in various ways, bear on the understanding of Chaucer.

Caxton printed *Reynard the Fox* twice [1481, 1488]. These charming stories of the sly fox, the noble lion, and their various companions in adventure and scheming have been endlessly reprinted and read, if not, as their Dutch Prologue, translated by Caxton, recommends, for profit, at least for pleasure.

III *Prose Romances*

Caxton's versions of Classical stories and his fables relate in some respects to the novel, which is usually not considered to have emerged as a formal genre until the eighteenth century in England. All of Caxton's narratives have some degree of the complex inter-relationship of plot episodes which is generally taken as the hallmark of the novel. Two prose romances, *Paris and Vienne* (1485) and *Blanchardin and Eglantine* [1488], are even more clearly in the general form of the novel, and Caxton himself translated as well as printed both works.

In *Paris and Vienne*, the title personages are young lovers separated by Vienne's father, who wishes to secure for her a profitable match. Her long and ingenious resistance to various suitors, together with Paris's great services to her father, finally unites the true lovers. The story is undistinguished in plot, characterization, or style; but the narrative demonstrates the interest readers have always taken in true love, particularly when its course contains disguise, intrigue, parental cruelty, and other such ordeals.

Much the same criticism may be made of *Blanchardin and Eglantine;* its narrative style is not lively, and its plot is long and tedious. Blanchardin, the son of a king and queen who had thought themselves destined to be childless, is not reared to perform deeds of war; but when he sees a tapestry of the Trojan War, he aspires to fight and consequently runs away from home. He is soon knighted by a man whose mortal wound and stolen lady he vows to avenge. Blanchardin does kill the villain and recover the lady, but she promptly dies of grief upon discovering that her knight is dead.

Blanchardin is so moved by the sight of her collapse upon the stomach of her lover that he breaks into a long declaration of his intention to pursue love himself and attaches his affections to Eglantine, a lady who has many suitors and a reputation for scorning them. Blanchardin finally wins both on the battlefield and in the lady's heart.

Although the plot is not strong, it can almost be said that in *Blanchardin and Eglantine,* episode is all. The characterization is often improbable and usually unimportant, and no significant statement issues from the events. The book's appearance in repeated editions testifies to its popularity,[11] but the popularity of such a book is no tribute to the general taste. More important than either *Paris and Vienne* or *Blanchardin and Eglantine,* however, is what Caxton says about the value to be derived from such reading. In the Prologue to *Blanchardin and Eglantine* he asserts that reading fiction can be commended:

[I] knew well that the story of hit was honest & joyful to all virtuous young noble gentlemen & women for to read therein as for their pastime; for under correction, in my judgment, it is as requisite other while [sometimes] to read in ancient histories of noble feats & valiant acts of arms & war which have been achieved in old time of many noble princes, lords, & knights, as well [as] for to see & know their valiantness for to stand in the special grace & love of their ladies, and in likewise for gentle young ladies & damoiselles for to learn to be steadfast & constant in their part to them that they once have promised and agreed to, such as have put their lives oft in jeopardy for to please them to stand in grace, as it is to occupy them and study over much in books of contemplation. (Crotch, p. 105)

While neither *Paris and Vienne* nor *Blanchardin and Eglantine* has the qualities of plot, theme, and character necessary to make it a great book, the recognition of the value of such reading "to pass the time" constitutes a step toward the acceptance of fiction in its own right—a step for which Caxton has been as much praised as he has been criticized for his unfortunate translation of *Eneydos.*[12]

IV *Caxton and the Christian Worthies*

Caxton had no need to translate the story of King Arthur, for a fifteenth century prose narrative of Arthur and his knights was readily available. Caxton's Prologue to Sir Thomas Malory's *Le Morte d'Arthur* (1485) tells how he decided to print it:

After that I had accomplished and finished diverse histories as well of contemplation as of other historical and worldly acts of great conquerors & princes, and also certain books of examples and doctrine, many noble and diverse gentlemen of this realm of England came and demanded me [asked me] many and oftentimes wherefore that I have not do made & enprint the noble history of the Saint Grail and of the most renowned Christian king, first and chief of the three best Christian and worthy, King Arthur, which ought most to be remembered among us English men tofore [before] all other Christian kings. For it is notoriously known through the universal world that there been ix worthy & the best that ever were. (Crotch p. 92)

Caxton then explains the Nine Worthies, three pagan—Hector, Alexander, and Julius Caesar; three Jewish—Joshua, David, and Judas Maccabaeus; and three Christian—Arthur, Charlemagne, and Godfrey of Bouillon (Caxton's spelling is Boloyne). He had already printed Godfrey's story, and

The said noble gentlemen [Caxton does not further identify them] instantly required me to emprint the history of the said noble king and conqueror King Arthur and of his knights, with the history of the Saint Grail, and of the death and ending of the said Arthur, affirming that I ought rather to enprint his acts and noble feats than of Godfrey of Boloyne or any of the other eight, considering that he was a man born within this realm and king and emperor of the same, and that there been in French diverse and many noble volumes of his acts, and also of his knights.

To whom I answered that diverse men hold opinion that there was no such Arthur and that all such books as been made of him been but feigned and fables, by cause that some chronicles make of him no mention nor remember [of] him no thing nor of his knights, whereto they answered, and one in special said that in him that should say or think that there was never such a king called Arthur might well be aretted [counted] great folly and blindness. For he said that there were many evidences of the contrary. First ye may see his sepulcher in the monastery of Glastonbury; and also in *Polychronicon*, in the v book, the sixth chapter, and in the seventh book, the xxiii chapter, where his body was buried and after found and translated to the said monastery. Ye shall see also in the history of Bochas [Boccaccio] in his book *De casu principum* [*De casibus virorum illustrium*] part of his noble acts and also of his fall; also Galfrydus in his Brutysshe book [Geoffrey of Monmouth in his British book, *Historia regum Britanniae*] recounteth his life; and in diverse places of England many remembrances been yet of him and shall remain perpetually, and also of his knights. First in the Abbey of Westminster at Saint Edward's shrine remaineth the print of his seal in red wax closed in beryl, in which is written *Patricius Arthurus, Britannie, Gallie, Germanie, Dacie, Imperator*. Item: in the Castle of Dover ye may see Gawain's skull &

Cradok's mantle; at Winchester the Round Table, in other places Lancelot's sword and many other things.

Then all these things considered, there can no man reasonably gainsay but there was a king of this land named Arthur. For in all places Christian and heathen he is reputed and taken for one of the ix worthy and the first of the three Christian men, and also he is more spoken of beyond the sea, more books made of his noble acts, than there be in England, as well in Dutch, Italian, Spanish, and Greek as in French. And yet of record remain in witness of him in Wales in the town of Camelot the great stones & marvellous works of iron lying under the ground, & royal vaults which diverse now living hath seen, wherefore it is a marvel why he is no more renowned in his own country, save only it accordeth to the word of God, which saith that no man is accept[ed] for a prophet in his own country.

Then all these things foresaid alleged I could not well deny but that there was such a noble king named Arthur and reputed one of the ix worthy & first & chief of the Christian men; & many noble volumes be made of him & of his noble knights in French which I have seen & read beyond the sea, which been not had in our maternal tongue; but in Welsh been many & also in French & some in English, but nowhere nigh all.

Wherefore such as have late been drawn out briefly into English, I have after the simple cunning that God hath sent to me, under the favor and correction of all noble lords and gentlemen enprysed [undertaken] to enprint a book of the noble histories of the said King Arthur and certain of his knights, after a copy unto me delivered, which copy Sir Thomas Malory did take out of certain books of French and reduced it into English. And I according to my copy have done set it in print, to the intent that noble men may see and learn the noble acts of chivalry, the gentle and virtuous deeds, that some knights used in those days, by which they came to honor; and how they that were vicious were punished and often put to shame and rebuke; humbly beseeching all noble lords and ladies and all other estates of what estate or degree they been of, that shall see and read in this said book and work, that they take the good and honest acts in their remembrance and to follow the same, wherein they shall find many joyous and pleasant histories and noble & renowned acts of humanity, gentleness, and chivalries. For herein may be seen noble chivalry, courtesy, humanity, friendliness, hardiness, love, friendship, cowardice, murder, hate, virtue, and sin. Do after the good and leave the evil, and it shall bring you to good fame and renown. And for to pass the time this book shall be pleasant to read in; but for to give faith and believe that all is true that is contained herein, ye be at your liberty; but all is written for our doctrine and for to beware that we fall not to vice ne sin, but t'exercise and follow virtue, by which we may come and attain to good fame and renown in this life, and after this short and transitory life to come unto everlasting bliss in heaven, the which He grant us that reigneth in heaven, the blessed Trinity. Amen. (Crotch, pp. 93–95)

Caxton equates the value of Arthur's story to its historicity; he states that the evidence alleged by his gentlemen-visitors persuaded him to print the book. But the Prologue expresses a remaining skepticism about the full historicity of the accounts of Arthur. Caxton also knows that a printed book ought to be edifying; he knows that not all the stories about Arthur and his knights are moral; and so he resorts to advising his readers to follow the good examples and to shun the bad ones, despite the fact that "all is written for our doctrine" (Crotch, p. 95), a biblical quotation which Chaucer before him had used to excuse naughty stories. Finally, the stories can be read for entertainment, "to pass the time" (Crotch, p. 95) pleasantly.

Insight into the significance of *Le Morte d'Arthur* can be gained through a comparison of the group of books which Caxton printed on the subject of the three Christian worthies: *Godfrey of Boloyne* (1481), a straight historical account in which fact is only moderately tempered by the author's point of view; *Charles the Great* (1485), a loose, rather aimless assortment of traditional materials assembled with some sense of dramatic development and coherence but lacking any distinct plot or theme; *Four Sons of Aymon* [1488], another Charlemagne romance which is somewhat more tightly constructed than *Charles the Great;* and *Le Morte d'Arthur*. It is useful to examine these four books in the order here given so as to observe the development of the prose narrative from factual history to fiction in the romance tradition which comes close to constituting the novel.

William of Tyre, whose dates are about 1130 to about 1190, became archbishop of Tyre in 1175. He wrote a Latin history which begins with the First Crusade, 1096–1099, and its immediately antecedent history and which is still regarded as a standard and reliable account. Caxton translated from a French version, somewhat modified, of William's *Historia rerum in partibus transmarinis gestarum,* concerned with Godfrey of Bouillon (1061?–1100).[13] Caxton's translation is called by various titles: *Godfrey of Boloyne* or *Siege and Conquest of Jerusalem* or, for the Roman Emperor Heraclius, *Eracles*. The first of these titles seems most clearly indicative of Caxton's intention to relate the story to one of the Christian worthies.[14]

In Caxton's translated portion of the history, William develops the story of the crusade through its various seiges, negotiations, and trials; and he finally comes to the crowning of Godfrey as king of Jerusalem. William deals bluntly with the difficulties of the crusaders. At the seige of Antioch, the scarcity of food, the high prices, and the prevalence of rain and death cause many to desert. Christians eat camels, asses, horses, dogs, and cats; and even cannibalism is reported. At Jerusalem, things are no better: heat, dust, and lack of water cause anguish as great as the hunger at Antioch. Beasts die, rot in the sun, and add the stench of their carcasses to the crusaders' grievous pain of thirst.

The valor and nobility of Godfrey contrast with the shame and suffering experienced during this crusade. The eldest of four valiant brothers, Godfrey is a devout man; and he honors good and religious men, keeps his word, scorns vanity, and is generous and kind. Although small in stature, he is remarkable for his strength and for the ease with which he bears his armor. In battle, he delivers a mighty blow which cuts an armor-clad Turk into two pieces, one of which falls to the ground while the other remains in the saddle. When it appears that Godfrey's chief vice is a too great love of going to church, he is elected king of Jerusalem; but his meekness and humility cause him to refuse to wear a king's crown in the city where Christ wore the crown of thorns. Godfrey lives to rule only a year.

Although William of Tyre's history is the result of conscientious, intelligent reporting, he is clearly so impressed by the contrast between the ignominious conduct of some of the crusaders and the virtue of Godfrey that he plays up the difference. In Caxton's translation, *Godfrey of Boloyne* is given focus and continuity because it isolates from William of Tyre's longer account a single central hero who is engaged in a single central action. Such selection can be part of the process by which fiction shapes unity from the diversity of life; but *Godfrey of Boloyne* remains historical and biographical, not fictional; for intelligence, sympathy, and judgment, but not imagination, have worked upon the material.

Caxton's Charlemagne stories are less factual than his *Godfrey,* less flattering to the hero, and generally less focused in plot. In Caxton's *Charles the Great,* which is divided into three books, the character of Charles is not favorably presented. He blusters and threatens, but his peers Oliver and Fierabras perform in a more creditable fashion. In Book I, the founding of the kingdom of France is traced back to one of Aeneas's companions, a man named Francus; the text names the holders of the French throne from Francus to Charles, and it then tells of Charles's succor of Jerusalem, whither he is led by a bird and whence he returns with miracle-working relics. Book II concerns a battle between Oliver, one of Charles's peers, and Fierabras, a gigantic and noble pagan who is eventually converted to Christianity, in a loose narrative which includes many attendant circumstances.

Book III deals with Charles's being led by a vision to emerge from retirement to rescue the shrine of St. James of Galicia from the Saracens. During his return to France, he loses Roland through the treachery of Ganelon, the story made famous in a different version in *The Song of Roland*. The sequence of events from book to book is governed by no discernible purpose.

In *Four Sons of Aymon*, Charles is even less great than in *Charles the Great*. In *Four Sons of Aymon*, which is one of the "rebel vassal" stories, the four sons—Reynawde, Alarde, Guichard and Richarde—fall into enmity with Charles and engage in a blood feud which sets father against sons. Charles's pettiness is best illustrated in the episode in which Reynawde surrenders his horse Bayard to Charles. When Charles has a stone fastened about Bayard's neck and casts him into a river, the narrative directs our response to the episode by its description of the grief of Charles's men at such cruelty. The compiler of *Four Sons of Aymon*, whoever he may have been, has escaped from the reverence for heroes that has often been dictated by history, but he has created a contradictory, not a complex, character. The extended length of *Four Sons of Aymon* and its prosaic style render it dull in manner and detail. In translating and in printing this story, Caxton contributed more to the history than to the grandeur of the chivalric romance.

Without Caxton's stories of Godfrey and Charles the Great, fifteenth century English literature would be different, but different chiefly in bulk. If Caxton's final reply to the "diverse gentlemen" who came to his shop to persuade him to print Malory's *Morte d'Arthur* had been "no," the shape of English literature would have been radically altered. We would have a heritage of Arthurian stories, to be sure, but not the long prose cradle-to-grave English narrative which *Le Morte d'Arthur* supplies. For four hundred and forty-nine years no fifteenth century text of Malory was known except Caxton's printed edition, and all subsequent editions of Malory were based on Caxton's.

Then, in 1934, W. F. Oakeshott discovered a fifteenth century Malory manuscript. Called the Winchester manuscript from the place of its discovery, it is judged by scholars to be neither a manuscript directly from Malory's hand nor one which he supervised. But even though the Winchester manuscript is not a definitive text, it offers an opportunity for comparing Caxton's version with that of another independent copy. Caxton's edition itself is extant in one perfect copy in the Morgan Library in New York City and in one damaged copy in the John Rylands Library in Manchester, England; these two copies contain a number of different readings. One of the miracles of modern printing has brought facsimile editions of both Caxton's Malory from the Morgan copy and the Winchester manuscript within reach of scholars.[15]

Readers have known from the beginning that Caxton exercised his judgment in editing *Le Morte d'Arthur;* for he states, in both Prologue and Epilogue, he has done so. The Epilogue reads:

Thus endeth this noble and joyous book entitled *Le Morte d'Arthur,* notwithstanding it treateth of the birth, life, and acts of the said King Arthur, of his noble knights of the Round Table, their marvellous enquestes [knightly ventures; *The Oxford English Dictionary* cites Malory and Caxton in *Blanchardin and Eglantine* as its first examples of this usage] and adventures, th' achieving of the Sangreal, and in th' end the dolorous death and departing out of this world of them all, which book was reduced into English by Sir Thomas Malory, knight, as afore is said, and by me divided into xxi books, chaptered and enprinted and finished in th' Abbey [of] Westminster the last day of July, the year of Our Lord MCCCClxxxv.
Caxton me fieri fecit.[16]

Comparison enables us to see how Caxton's printed text differs from the Winchester manuscript; although it does not enable us to determine precisely what Caxton's own manuscript contained, we can examine with profit some of the differences between the Winchester and Caxton texts. Caxton's comment in the Epilogue that *Le Morte d'Arthur* embraces the whole life of Arthur and his knights suggests that the narrative is a continuous if somewhat episodic whole. The Winchester manuscript contains eight *explicits,* or end notes, which bring the work to a series of conclusions. Warm debate exists among scholars over the question of whether Malory meant to provide one unified work or a series of separate tales.[17] It is evident that Caxton, if he worked from a manuscript with the full eight explicits and their possible implication of the division of the text into separate tales, chose to treat the matter as one tale.

Turning eight tales into one would constitute a major editorial decision, one well beyond the division of the material into books and chapters. A comparison of a short passage from the two versions shows also the frequent small differences which exist between the two editions. The passages quoted come from folio 148, v, in Winchester and from Book VIII, Chapter 1, in Caxton.[18] The "W" in the left margin indicates the Winchester text; the "C," the Caxton:

W   Here begynnyth the fyrste boke of Syr Tristrams
C   Here foloweth the viij book the which is the first book of sir Tristram

W   de lyones and who was his fadir and hys modyr and how he
C   de Lyones/& who was his fader & his moder/& hou he

W   was borne and fostyrd and how he was made knyght of Kynge Marke of
    Cornuayle
C   was borne and fosteryd / And how he was made knyghte

W   There was a kynge that hyght Melyodas and he was lorde
C   Hit was a kyng that hyghte Melyodas / and he was lord

W   of the contrey of lyones and this Melyodas was
C   and kynge of the countre of Lyonas And this Melyodas was

W   a lykly knyght as ony was p^t tyme lyvyng and by fortune
C   a lykely knyght as ony was that tyme lyuynge / And by fortune

W   he wedded kynge Markis sist of Cornuayle and she was
C   he wedded kynge Markys syster of Cornewaille / And she was

W   called Elyzabeth that was called bothe good and fayre and
C   called Elyzabeth that was callyd bothe good and fair And

W   at that tyme kynge Arthure regned and he was hole kynge
C   at that tyme kynge Arthur regned / and he was hole kynge

W   of Ingelonde. Walys . Scotlonde and of many othir realmys
C   of Englond / walys and Scotland & of many other royammes

W   how be hit p^r were many kynges that were lordys of many
C   how be it there were many kynges that were lordes of many

W   countreyes But all they helde p^r londys of kynge Arthure
C   countreyes / but alle they held their landes of kyng Arthur/

W   ffor in Walys were ·ii· kynges and in the Northe were many kynges
C   for in walys were two kynges/and in the north were many kynges/

W   and in Cornuayle and in the weste were ·ii· kynges. Also
C   And in Cornewail and in the west were two kynges / ¶ Also

W   in Irelonde were ·ii· or ·iii· kynges and all were undir the
C   in Irland were two or thre kynges and al were vnder the

W   obeysaunce of kynge Arthure so was pᵉ kynge of ffraunce
C   obeissaunce of kyng Arthur / So was the kynge of Fraunce

W   and the kyng of Bretayne and all the lordshyppis unto Roome /
C   and the kyng of Bretayn and all the lordshippes vnto Rome /

Caxton's text is slightly more modern than the Winchester: Winchester uses the old character p (thorn) where Caxton prints *th*. It uses contractions such as pʳ for *there* or pᵉ for *the*. Neither is heavily punctuated, but Caxton's virgule (/) provides a useful clue to syntax. The spelling in the two versions differs, but the twentieth century reader would find it difficult to choose between them for spelling preferences. Caxton cannot resist the impulse to use doublets: "lord" becomes "lord and king."

In studying the two versions of Malory, however, it becomes apparent that the essential change which Caxton makes is not in details: lordys, lordes; helde, held; londys, laudes. Rather, it is in Caxton's large excisions in the account of Arthur and the Emperor Lucius. The extent and nature of these changes—ones too extensive to quote—can be most readily perceived by examining the Emperor Lucius story in the edition by Eugène Vinaver[19] which gives the Winchester text at the top of each page and the Caxton version on the lower portion. Caxton has clearly exerted a great editorial effort in compressing the material.

The editor's duty of fidelity to a text sat somewhat lightly upon Caxton as he edited Malory, perhaps because he had reservations about the book. Caxton's various prologues and epilogues indicate that he valued factuality, edification, diversion, and style. His Prologue to *Le Morte d'Arthur* asserts that he had been persuaded that Arthur is an historical figure, but his full belief in the stories clustered around Arthur can hardly be asserted. The Prologue directs attention to the possible moral profit to be gained from reading *Le Morte*—if the reader follows the good examples and not the evil ones. Caxton recommends the book for pleasure reading; but on the subject of fair language, his Prologue is silent.

The case can also be made that Caxton's alterations of *Le Morte d'Arthur* are in harmony with Malory's own efforts. Malory's explicits indicate that he wished to make the vast body of Arthurian lore conveniently available to English readers, and he was concerned with controlling the mass and shape of his materials. In his punctuation and spelling, designed to give recognizable shape to words and sentences, in his divisions of material into books and chapters, and deletions, Caxton seems to have had the same goal of forcing the material into comprehensible form. A twentieth century editor who uses modern spelling and punctuation and who divides sentences and paragraphs in conformity to contemporary practice is doing precisely the same thing that Caxton did, and for the same reason.

Although Malory's *Le Morte d'Arthur* is composed from a great body of disparate materials, it achieves a central focus: a group of peers sworn to a common goal gather in a circle around a common table and serve a central and peerless leader. When Arthur takes unworthy actions, as in the begetting of Mordred, who eventually kills his father, and when, for the peerless but mortal leader Arthur, the knights substitute the peerless and immortal quest of the Grail, the temporal circle of the Round Table is broken. Arthur is a hero, but he is not the ultimate hero, and the fact that he can be equaled or bettered by deeply flawed Lancelot demonstrates that lack. There is an archetypal, unified, and significant theme in *Le Morte d'Arthur*. We cannot claim preternatural perceptions for Caxton; but when he called Malory's book *Le Morte d'Arthur*, he made no mistake. The book is not *King Arthur and His Knights of the Round Table;* it is *The Death of Arthur*, the end of a temporal ideal, the death of chivalry.

Le Morte d'Arthur has the simple and incontrovertible evidence of a host of readers to testify to its success, despite the failure of Malory and Caxton to make it a perfect book. It is better than *The Recuyell of the Historyes of Troye* because it has its materials under better control; better than *Jason* or *Charles the Great* because it has found a more significant theme; better than *Four Sons of Aymon* because it draws less fixed and arbitrary lines between good and evil—Malory can work with amphibologies. It is better as a story, though not as history, than *Godfrey of Boloyne* because the storyteller can select and shape material as the historian must not.

Le Morte d'Arthur is too long; too many knights trase and traverse and foyne too many times. But it is an effective story; it is, as Caxton knew, a story of "the knowledge of good . . . involved and interwoven with the knowledge of evil"[20] and redeemable only in death; a story with a moral; perhaps a story made from history; but a story.

V   *Caxton and the English Poets*

Whereas Caxton translated all the prose narratives he printed except *Le Morte d'Arthur*, he made few attempts to write in rhyme;

for he utilized prose translations even of poetic texts. That he
admired poetry is evidenced by the fact that he printed verse
narratives by three great English poets: Geoffrey Chaucer, John
Gower, and John Lydgate. It is illuminating to begin with the latest in
time and with the least significant in achievement of the three, John
Lydgate. Accident more than choice may have determined Caxton's
selections from Lydgate, which are several small pieces, not the now
famous long works. Caxton printed Lydgate's *The Churl and the Bird*
twice [1476 and 1477 or 1478]. In this fable, a commonly told one, the
bird instructs the churl and draws two conclusions—that wisdom can
be taught through feigned matters, and that the churl is too deeply set
in his ignorance to profit by wisdom.

A second Lydgate poem printed by Caxton is a debate entitled
The Horse, Sheep, and Goose, which Caxton also printed twice [1476
and 1477 or 1478]. In it, the horse, the goose, and the sheep debate
their respective utility to man. An eagle and a lion serve as judges,
and the conclusion is that each creature has its contribution to make.
The poem is followed by a lament for the decay of the world; by a
piece of advice to all estates, or classes, to be content with their lots;
and by a list of names for several of a kind of certain animals—a herd of
harts, a seige of herons, and so on. How such an assortment of
materials was rationalized in the compiler's mind is neither stated nor
apparent.

Among the Lydgate works published by Caxton, Lydgate's debt to
Chaucer appears most clearly in *The Temple of Glass* [1477 or 1478].
The poem is a dream vision of a temple of glass whose walls depict
thousands of lovers. After Lydgate tells some of their stories briefly,
he discusses one pair of lovers in some detail. When this pair is united
by Venus, the dreamer wakens and sends the book to his own lady.
Long accounts of how a lover should behave make the poem a sort of
lovers' courtesy book. *The Temple of Glass* lacks the quality of
language, imagery, or imagination that makes a poem into poetry, but
it may have attracted fifteenth century readers as a repository of
romantic material. Its chief abiding interest is its double tribute to
Chaucer, through its imitation in form and matter of Chaucer's *House
of Fame* and through Lydgate's references to Chaucer, which are
scattered throughout the poem.

Lydgate is one of the poets recommended in *The Book of Courtesy*,
which Caxton printed (see Chapter 1). Lydgate's own little courtesy
book for children, *Stans puer ad mensam*, has been discussed in
Chapter 5, and *The Pilgrimage of the Soul*, no longer attributed to

Lydgate, in Chapter 4. Caxton's Epilogue to Book II of his own prose translation of *The Recuyell of the Historyes of Troye* speaks at some length of Lydgate's translation of Book III of *The Recuyell:* "And as for the third book which treateth the general & last destruction of Troy, hit needeth not to translate hit into English, for as much as that worshipful & religious man, Dan John Lydgate, monk of Bury, did translate hit but late, after whose work I fear to take upon me that am not worthy to bear his penner [pencase] and inkhorn after him to meddle in that work" (Crotch, p. 6). Caxton then offers various reasons for continuing his own prose translation: "[Lydgate's] work is in rhyme, and as far as I know hit [Book III of *The Recuyell*] is not had in prose in our tongue, and also paradventure [perhaps] he translated after some other author than this is, and yet for as much as diverse men been of diverse desires, some to read in rhyme and meter and some in prose, and also because I have now good leisure . . ." (Crotch, p. 7). Caxton completed and printed his own three book prose translation of *The Recuyell of the Historyes of Troye;* but he did not print Lydgate's *Troy Book*. However, Caxton did print one other poem by Lydgate, a long verse account of the Virgin Mary called *The Life of Our Lady* [1483], a compendium of general Medieval traditions concerning Mary.

Like Lydgate, John Gower owes part of his current reputation to his association with Chaucer, for they were London contemporaries and friends. Gower wrote three major poems, all long narratives, one in Latin, one in French, and one in English. Caxton printed the English poem, *Confessio amantis*, or *The Lover's Confession* (1483),[21] in which a lover, bidden to confess his sins against love, replies that he must be instructed in the nature of these sins in order to examine himself for guilt. After the priest, Genius, explains the entrance of love through the senses, especially sight, he enumerates the Seven Deadly Sins that are only ostensibly against love, he cites their multifarious branches and opposite virtues, and he illustrates them with a plentitude of stories.

Gower's Prologue announces his intention to blend instruction and entertainment. To that end, he draws upon the whole complex of Medieval interests. He is both encyclopedic and digressive: war, the crusades, inventions of all kinds, alchemy, sorcery, education, geography, astronomy, and Dame Fortune—all find their way into the tales. Finally, the lover is bidden to turn his love to God, and the poem ends with a prayer for England in which the poet expresses the hope that all classes will devote themselves to the cause of peace.

Gower's *Confessio amantis* is always paired with *The Canterbury Tales* as an example of the "frame story" which embraces a host of short narratives. Since Gower's illustrative narratives are not in the main well developed or lively, they are more comparable in quality to the narratives in Chaucer's *Legend of Good Women* than to those in his *Canterbury Tales.*

Three facts make Caxton's editing of Chaucer the most instructive basis for assessing his qualities as an editor: Caxton printed more of Chaucer's work than of any other single writer's; he commented on his own perceptions of Chaucer's worth; and since Chaucer is the English Medieval writer whose reputation is currently highest, his works' popularity provides a means of setting Caxton's views in balance against those of later critics who may be no wiser but who have at least the advantage of accumulated judgment in the shaping of their own views.

When Caxton printed Chaucer's charming bird fable, *The Parliament of Fowls* [1477 or 1478] and his rather slight *Anelida*, together with *Chaucer to his Empty Purse* and *Envoy to the King* [1477 or 1478], he made no comment on these editions. Caxton also printed Chaucer's translation of *Boethius de consolatione philosophiae* which is not a poem but which afforded Caxton an opportunity to praise Chaucer as a stylist. Boethius, Caxton says, "was an excellent author of diverse books craftily and curiously made in prose and meter," but:

for as much as [since] the style . . . is hard & difficult to be understood of simple persons, therefore the worshipful father & first founder & embellisher of ornate eloquence in our English, I mean Master Geoffrey Chaucer, hath translated this said work out of Latin into our usual and mother tongue, following the Latin as nigh as is possible to be understood, wherein in mine opinion he hath deserved a perpetual laud and thank of all this noble Realm of England, and in especial of them that shall read & understand it. . . . And furthermore I desire & require you that of your charity ye would pray for the soul of the said worshipful man Geoffrey Chaucer, first translator of this said book into English & embellisher in making the said language ornate & fair, which shall endure perpetually, and therefore he ought eternally to be remembered. (Crotch, pp. 36-37)

Caxton then states that Chaucer is buried in Westminster Abbey and quotes a Latin "Epitaph made by a poet laureate." Caxton concludes his Epilogue to *Boethius:*

Post obitum Caxton voluit te viuere cura
Willelmi. Chaucer clare poeta tuj

> Nam tua non solum compressit opuscula formis
> Has quoque suas laudes . iussit hic esse tuas. (Crotch, p. 37)

The lines may be translated: "After death, Caxton [wishes] you to live by your William's care, Chaucer, noble poet. For none but he has printed your work in [proper] form; and these his praises also he directs to become yours."[22]

When Caxton printed Chaucer's *Book of Fame* [1483], a dream vision which in all known manuscripts is incomplete, he supplied a conclusion by means of a few lines of his own composition. These lines, which are marked in the margin with Caxton's name, say that the dreamer was awakened by a great clamor and so can relate no more of the events of the dream:

> And with the noise of them wo[Blake amends *wo* to *two*]
> I suddenly awoke anon tho [immediately then]
> And remembered what I had seen
> And how high and far I had been
> In my ghost [spirit] and had great wonder
> Of that the god of thunder
> Had let me knowen and began to write
> Like as ye have heard me endyte [say]
> Wherefore to study and read alway
> I purpose to do day by day.
> Thus in dreaming and in game
> Endeth this little book of Fame.[23]

Caxton's Epilogue states his reasons for believing the poem worth printing even though it is incomplete:

I find no more of this work. . . . For as far as I can understand, this noble man Geoffrey Chaucer finished at the said conclusion [at the conclusion as printed in Caxton's text prior to his own addition] . . . which work as me seemeth [as it seems to me] is craftily made and digne [worthy] to be written & known. For he toucheth in it right great wisdom & subtle understanding. And so in all his works he excelleth in mine opinion all other writers in our English. For he writeth no void words, but all his matter is full of high and quick [living] sentence [wisdom], to whom ought to be given laud and praising for his noble making and writing. For of him all other have borrowed since and taken, in all their well saying and writing. (Crotch, p. 69)

Caxton printed an edition of *The Canterbury Tales* [1478] and one of *Troilus and Criseyde* [1483] without any comment of his own concerning them. But when he printed a second edition of *The Canterbury Tales* [1483], he presented a detailed account of how he came to do so:

Great thanks, laud, and honor ought to be given unto the clerks, poets, and historiographs [*The Oxford English Dictionary* shows Caxton's *Game and Play of the Chess* as its first example in English of "historiograph," meaning historical writer] that have written many noble books of wisdom, of the lives, passions, & miracles of holy saints, of histories and of noble and famous acts and feats, and of chronicles since the beginning of the creation of the world unto this present time, by which we been daily informed and have knowledge of many things of whom [of which] we should not have known if they had not left to us their monuments written.

Among whom and in especial to fore [before] all other we ought to give a singular laud unto that noble & great philosopher Geoffrey Chaucer, the which for his ornate writing in our tongue may well have the name of a laureate poet. For to fore that he by his labor embellished, ornated, and made fair our English, in this Realm was had rude speech & incongrue [incongruous], as it yet appeareth by old books which at this day ought not to have place nor be compared among nor to his beauteous volumes and aournate [ornate] writings, of whom [of which] he made many books and treatises of many a noble history as well in meter as in rhyme and prose, and them so craftily made that he comprehended [included, contained] his matters in short, quick [living], and high sentences, eschewing prolixity, casting away the chaff of superfluity, and showing the picked [selected] grain of sentence [wisdom] uttered by crafty [artistic] and sugared eloquence, of whom [of which] among all other of his books I purpose t'imprint by the grace of God the book of *The Tales of Canterbury*, in which I find many a noble history of every estate and degree, first rehearsing the conditions and th'array of each of them as properly as possible is to be said [Caxton is here paraphrasing Chaucer's own *General Prologue* to *The Canterbury Tales*] and after their tales which been of nobleness, wisdom, gentleness, mirth, and also of verray [true] holiness and virtue, wherein he finisheth this said book.

Which book I have diligently overseen and duly examined to th'end that it be made according unto his own making. For I find many of the said books [many copies of these books] which writers [copyists] have abridged it and many things left out, and in some place have set certain verses that he never made nor set in his book, of which books so incorrect was one brought to me vj year passed, which I supposed had been verray [true], true, & correct, and according to the same I did do imprint a certain number of them, which anon were sold to many and diverse gentlemen, of whom one gentleman came to me and said that this book was not according in many places unto the book that Geoffrey Chaucer had made. To whom I answered that I had made it according to my copy, and by me was nothing added nor minished [diminished, taken away]. Then he said he knew a book which his father had and much loved, that was very true and according unto his own first book by him made, and said more, if I would enprint it again he would get me the same book for a copy, howbeit he wist [knew] well that his father would not gladly depart [part] from it. To whom I said, in case that he could get me such a book, true and correct, yet I would once endeavor me to enprint it again, for to satisfy th'author, whereas to fore by ignorance I erred in hurting and defaming his book in diverse places, in setting in some things that he never said nor made, and leaving out many things that he made which been requisite to be set in it.

And thus we fell at accord. And he full gently [most courteously] got of his father the said book and delivered it to me, by which I have corrected my book, as hereafter all along by th'aid of Almighty God shall follow, whom I humble beseech to give me grace and aid to achieve and accomplish to his laud, honor, and glory, and that all ye that shall in this book read or hear, will of your charity among your deeds of mercy, remember the soul of the said Geoffrey Chaucer, first author and maker of this book. And also that all we that shall see and read therein may so take and understand the good and virtuous tales that it may so profit unto the health of our souls, that after this short and transitory life we may come to everlasting life in heaven. Amen. (Crotch, pp. 90–91)

This Prologue tells us several things. First, it sets Chaucer in high company—among the historians and the philosophers who are capable of assisting man to salvation. Second, it testifies to Caxton's love of Chaucer for his style. Third, it tells us that Caxton wishes to produce a faithful text. Fourth and finally, it indicates how uncertain and unreliable the manuscripts from which Caxton might have to work could be.

Since Caxton felt compelled to correct his own first edition of *The Canterbury Tales*, it is instructive to examine what he achieved in a second edition.[24] We cite, for this purpose, the text of the most familiar part of the poem, the opening eighteen lines of the *General Prologue;* in each pair, the text of Caxton's first edition is first and the text of Caxton's second edition follows:

Line 1   Whan that Apprill with his shouris sote
          Whan that Apryll wyth hys shouris sote

Line 2   And the droughte of marche hath pcid p^e rote
          The droughte of marche hath percyd the rote

Line 3   And badid euery veyne in suche licour
          And bathyd euery veyne in suche lycour

Line 4   Of whiche vertu engendrid is the flour
          Of whyche vertue engendryd is the flour

Line 5   Whanne zepherus eke with his sote breth
          Whanne Zepherus eke wyth hys sote breth

Line 6   Enspirid hath in euery holte and heth
          Enspyrid hath in euery holte and heth

Line 7   The tendir croppis and the yong sonne
          The tendyr croppis / and the yong sonne

Line 8   Hath in the ram half his cours y ronne
          Hath in the ram half hys cours y ronne

Line 9   And smale foulis make melodie
          And smale foulis make melodye

Line 10   That slepyn al nyght with opyn ye
          That slepyn al nyght wyth opyn eye

Line 11   So prikith hem nature in her corage
          So prykyth hem nature in her corages

Line 12   Than longyng folk to gon on pilgremage
          Than longyn folk to gon on pylgremages

Line 13   And palmers to seche straunge londis
          And palmers to seche straunge strondis

Line 14   To serue halowis conthe in sondry londis
          To serue halowys couthe in sondry londis

Line 15   And specially fro euery shiris ende
          And specyally fro euery shyris ende

Line 16   Of yngelond to Cauntirbury thy wende
          Of engelond to Cauntirbury thy wende

Line 17   The holy blisful martir forto seke
          The holy blysful martir for to seke

Line 18   That them hath holpen when they were seke
          That them hath holpyn when they were seke

The inverted letter in Line 14 that gives "conthe," corrected to "couthe" (know), is one of Caxton's commonest typographical errors; it occurs even in his own name. Comparison of these lines to a modern edition reveals a few alterations of meaning in Caxton's text in both editions. In Line 14, what should be "ferne" appears as "serve," so that "to distant shrines" has become "to serve shrines." In Line 16, "they" is given as "thy," an error Caxton's readers would have had to correct for themselves in order to understand the line. The spelling of "hem" in Line 18 as "them" removes the alliteration of the three successive *h*'s which Chaucer wrote into the line, but it does not affect the general meaning. The second edition recovers the alliteration in Line 13 by altering "straunge londis" to "straunge strondis."

Certain spelling variations are unimportant—yngelond, engelond; blisful, blysful—but others are significant because they alter the rhythm. The omission of "to" in Line 2 alters both rhythm and sense. Perhaps more common that the additions and omissions of words, however, is the unChaucerian handling of final *e*'s. A final *e*, which to Caxton and to modern English speakers has become a "silent" *e*, is metrically significant in Chaucer. The *e*'s, remnants of old endings which had grammatical content, generally count as unstressed syllables in the meter of Chaucer's lines with the sound value of *a* in about. The omission of an *e* on yong in Line 7 and the additions of *e*'s in Lines 4 and 5, for example, and also the alteration of the *es* to *s* on palmeres, with the resultant loss of a syllable, would interfere seriously with the apprehension of Chaucer's musical qualities.

In Caxton's defense, however, two points must be recalled: First, the pronunciation of the final *e* was dying in Chaucer's day, and Caxton could hardly have realized that he was altering more than the spelling of words when he added or deleted these *e*'s. If he had given them correctly, he and his contemporaries would not have used them as clues to rhythm. Second, there is no perfect surviving manuscript. An examination of the textual notes in one of the modern editions of *The Canterbury Tales* reveals how many, and sometimes how unsure, are the editorial decisions which must be made today. Caxton had to deal as best he could with a somewhat unreliable text even in his second edition. The fact that, when offered a better manuscript, he undertook a second edition testifies to his desire to do well by Chaucer.

The second edition did not altogether succeed since numerous

errors were carried into it from the first edition. An examination of
some lines, again from the *General Prologue*—this time from the
description of the Friar—shows that a major revision was necessary if
the sequence of lines is to make sense. Again, the first line in each of
the pairs is from the first edition; the second, from the second edition:

Line 1   A Frere ther was awanton & a mery
          A Frere ther was awanton and a mery

Line 2   A lymytour and a ful solemne man
          A lymytour and a ful solemne man

Line 3   In alle the ordris four is non that so wel can
          In alle the ordrys four is non that can

Line 4   So moche of daliaunce and fair langage
          So moche of daliaunce and fair langage

Line 5   He hadde made meny a fair mariage
          He hadde made ful many a fair mariage

Line 6   Of yonge wommen at his owen cost
          Of yong wymmen at hys owen cost

Line 7   Vntil his ordre he was an nobil post
          Vntil hys ordre he was a nobil post

Line 8   Ful welbeloued and ful famulier was he
          Ful welbeloued and ful famylier was he

Line 9   With frankeleyns ouer al in his contre
          With frankeleyns ouer al in his contre

Line 10   And with worthy yemen of the toun
          And eke wyth worthy yemen of the toun

Line 11   For he hadde power of confession
          For he had power of confession

Line 12   And plesaunt was his absolucion
          As sayd hym self more than a curat

Line 13   To them that had grete contricion
          And of hys ordre he was licenciat

Line 14   And sayde hym self more than a curat
           Ful swetly herd he confession

Line 15   And of his ordre he was licenciat
           And plesaunt was hys absolucion

Line 16   And an esi man to yeue penaunce
           And an esy man to gyue penaunce

Line 17   There he wiste to haue good pitaunce
           There he wyste to haue good pitaunce

Line 18   Vnto a poure ordre forto yeue
           For vnto a poure ordre forto gyue

Line 19   Whan that a man is wel J shryue
           Is signe that a man is wel j shryue

Line 20   Yf he yaf he durste make avaunt
           For yf he yaf/he durste make a vaunt

Line 21   Yf that a man was repentaunt
           He wyst that a man was repentaunt

In addition to the sequence of the lines, the quotation shows some of
the alterations in details between the first and second editions. In
keeping the "yeomen" of Line 10, Caxton loses not only the
alliteration that "women" would have given but also the implication
of the Friar's affection for ladies, of course.

    Chaucer's *The Canterbury Tales*, like *The Book of Fame*, was never
completed; and, being a series of tales in a narrative framework, it
lends itself to argument about the order in which the existing tales
should appear. The order is determined chiefly by the headlinks and
endlinks, the words exchanged among the pilgrims at the beginnings
and ends of tales. In certain places, however, these do not appear
or—perhaps even worse for the editor—do not give clear directions.
Two courses are open: to follow the order of a particular manuscript or
to try to arrive at an order by some internal logic.[25] In the second
edition, Caxton not only corrected his text line by line but attempted
to arrive at a better sequence of tales; but the order he uses is not, in
either edition, of any signal merit.

    Caxton's order in the first edition is: Knight, Miller, Reeve, Cook,
Man of Law, Squire, Merchant, Wife of Bath, Friar, Summoner,

Clerk, Franklin, Second Nun, Canon's Yeoman, Physician, Par-
doner, Shipman, Prioress, Sir Thopas, Melibeus, Monk, Nun's
Priest, Manciple, Parson. In the second edition: Knight, Miller,
Reeve, Cook, Man of Law, Merchant, Squire, Franklin, Wife of
Bath, Friar, Summoner, Clerk, Second Nun, Canon's Yeoman,
Physician, Pardoner, Shipman, Prioress, Sir Thopas, Melibeus,
Monk, Nun's Priest, Manciple, Parson. Each edition concludes with
the Retraction.

Among the improvements which Caxton introduced into his
second edition of *The Canterbury Tales* is a set of woodcuts. A
woodcut of the pilgrim usually appears at the place where he is
described in the *General Prologue* and at the beginning of his tale, but
the likeness may not fit the impression of the pilgrim which rises from
the text. The second edition also adds running titles for the Prologues
and Tales. All in all, however, Caxton's second edition of *The
Canterbury Tales* falls short of being either textually perfect or
visually attractive. Perhaps the greatest value of the second edition,
in fact, is that it caused Caxton to write a long Prologue which
expresses his admiration for Chaucer.

Since Chaucer is too well known to require synopsis and too great
to be dealt with summarily, the point that needs to be made here is
that although Chaucer uses the same materials and techniques that
were used by other writers of verse and prose narratives which were
printed by Caxton, Chaucer makes something different from them.
Confessio amantis and *The Canterbury Tales* constitute two
framework narratives; but whereas *Confessio amantis* has only an
obvious but superficial unity through its concentration on the sins
against love, *The Canterbury Tales* has a transcendant unity which
rises from the wholeness and soundness of the artist's vision. *The
Recuyell of the Historyes of Troye* sets out to be faithful to the story of
Troy. *Troilus and Criseyde*, also a Trojan War story, sets out to be
faithful to the human experience. Its characters, events, and themes
speak without respect to time or place of the verifiable experiences
and the irresistible aspirations of the human race. Only *Reynard the
Fox*, at its own less ambitious level, approaches Chaucer's accomplishment.

The ultimate measure of Caxton as an editor is that he chose to
publish Chaucer and that he endeavored to issue an authoritative
text. In Chaucer he had found the genius which projects character in
its full dimension and complexity, which makes symbols embody
their own truth, which selects and orders details so as to create

wholeness, which transforms fact into perception, and which makes language one of mankind's signal arts. Caxton could not have said of Chaucer all that twentieth century scholarship has found to say. But he knew genius when he encountered it, and he used the press to help stories survive and accomplish their ends.

As Higden's *Polychronicon* declares, "Writing of poets is more worth to praising of emperors than all the wealth of this world and riches that they wielded [controlled] while they were alive. For story is witness of time, mind of life, messenger of oldness. Story wieldeth passing doings, story putteth forth her professors. Deeds that would be lost story reneweth; deeds that would flee out of mind, story calleth again; deeds that would die, story keepeth them evermore" (folio v, r–v).

CHAPTER 7

Caxton's Prose Style

CAXTON'S place as an author rests upon his work as a translator and essayist; and, indeed, his extensive translations to a great degree furnished the English prose accessible to the mass market from 1475 to 1491.[1] We need, therefore, to consider Caxton as a stylist through the analysis of representative passages from his translations and from his free composition and through an analysis of what he himself had to say about his method of translation and his sense of style.

I Three Periods

Since Caxton completed the translation of *The Recuyell of the Historyes of Troye* in 1471 and printed it about 1475, translated and presumably also printed *Reynard the Fox* in 1481, and completed *Eneydos* in 1490, these three works provide a means of looking at Caxton's prose in his early, middle, and late years and, through the use of both prologues and texts, of examining both his free composition and his translation.

The Recuyell of the Historyes of Troye contains the first known example of Caxton's literary style. Its Prologue, which is in part a translation, demonstrates that both Caxton's vocabulary and his syntax are subject to the shaping influence of the material he translated. In each of the sets of three lines which follow, the first line is from Raoul Lefèvre's French, the second is from Caxton, and the third is my modernization of Caxton:

Cy commence le volume
hEre begynneth the volume
Here begins the volume

Intitule   le recueil   des histoires de troyes
intituled and named the recuyell of the historyes of Troye/
entitled and named the collection of the histories of Troy,

Compose
composed and drawen out of dyuerce bookes of latyn in to frensshe
composed and drawn out of various books in Latin into French

par   venerable   homme
by the ryght venerable persone and worshipfull man.
by the right venerable person and worshipful man,

raoul le feure prestre chappellain
Raoul de ffeure. preest and chapelayn
Raoul Lefèvre, priest and chaplain

de mon tresredonte seigneur Monseigneur
vnto the ryght noble gloryous and myghty prynce in his tyme
to the right noble, glorious, and mighty prince in his time,

le Duc Phelippe de bourgoingne
Phelip duc of Bourgoyne of Braband etc
Philip, Duke of Burgundy, of Brabant, etc.

En   lan de grace.
In the yere of the Incarnacion of our lord god
in the year of the incarnation of Our Lord God

mil.   .cccc.   .lxiiii.:.
a thousand foure honderd sixty and foure/
a thousand four hundred and sixty-four. . . .[2]

In his own lines, Caxton thriftily utilizes Raoul Lefèvre's opening
statement as his own, though not without some ornamentation.
Caxton can gracefully call Lefèvre not merely "venerable" but a
"right venerable person and worshipful man," a compliment Lefèvre
would hardly pay himself. Lefèvre's description of Philip, "tresredonte seigneur Monseigneur"—"very redoubtable lord, His
Lordship"—becomes the more extravagant, "right noble, glorious,
and mighty prince in his time." From the beginning, Caxton's bent is
toward the elaborate, the ornate, the verbose. However, Lefèvre
himself is only biding his time; in a few lines, he begins to praise
Philip, but Caxton makes his own statement about Philip early in

order to have space for the praise of Margaret of Burgundy which he adds (see below).

As Caxton continues the sentence already quoted, he begins constructing his own prose (from this point on, quotations from Caxton in this chapter, in conformity to the general usage in this book, are spelled, punctuated, capitalized, and paragraphed in conformity to modern practice, but with close fidelity to Caxton's vocabulary and sentence structure; archaic and obsolete words are noted in brackets; some of them cast interesting light on modern usages):

and translated and drawn out of French into English by William Caxton, mercer, of the city of London, at the commandment of the right high, mighty, and virtuous princess, his redoubted lady, Margaret, by the grace of God, Duchess of Burgundy, of Lotryk, of Brabant, etc., which said translation and work was begun in Bruges in the country of Flanders, the first day of March, the year of the incarnation of our said Lord God a thousand four hundred sixty and eight, and ended and finished in the holy city of Cologne the .xix. day of September, the year of our said Lord God a thousand four hundred sixty and eleven, etc. (Crotch, p. 2).

Analyzing Medieval syntax involves a problem which modern English does not: we cannot be sure where sentences begin and end. Medieval punctuation is light; Caxton most frequently uses a virgule (/) and employs it as we would use both the comma and the period. His "which" sometimes equates to the modern usage of "this." He sometimes uses verbs with no subject expressed, a carryover from a more fully inflected stage of the language when the pronoun subject could be expressed in the inflectional ending of a verb. Caxton begins the phrase "Which said translation . . ." and also the phrase "And ended and finished . . ." with capital letters. We might, therefore, construe the matter quoted here as containing, not one, but three sentences, with the second beginning at "Which" and the third at "And."[3] The problem is, fortunately, more apparent than real since the movement of the thought is not significantly altered by our concept of the precise sentence units. Three points in the material quoted are linked together by content: "translated . . . by William Caxton"; "Which said translation . . . was begun"; "And ended. . . ." In spite of intervening phrases, the connectives which and and serve to link the parts together.

Caxton often employs pairs of synonyms or doublets: entitled and

named, composed and drawn out; translation and work. To him,
translated will not suffice where translated and drawn out are
available, or ended for ended and finished. The three dates are
expressed in more words than the simple sense requires, and etc.
seems to be used as an ornamental flourish; it does not refer to any
specific omitted content. When Caxton wishes simply to state a fact,
however, he can construct a direct, simple sentence: "And on that
other side of this leaf followeth the prologue" (Crotch, p. 2).

Although Raoul Lefèvre's Prologue provides Caxton a model for
the remainder of his own Prologue, Caxton's contains a circumstantial
account of how he translated and printed *The Recuyell*. I construe the
following passage, the opening of the second Prologue, which follows
the one already quoted, as a single sentence:

When I remember that every man is bounden by the commandment &
counsel of the wise man to eschew sloth and idleness, which is mother and
nourisher of vices, and ought to put myself unto virtuous occupation and
business, then I, having no great charge of occupation, following the said
counsel, took a French book and read therein many strange and marvellous
histories, wherein I had great pleasure and delight, as well for the novelty of
the same as for the fair language of French, which was in prose so well and
compendiously [concisely] set and written, which me thought I understood
the sentence and substance of every matter. (Crotch, p. 4)

Since traditional grammar works well for the problem we need to
tackle, I analyze this passage by using traditional terminology.[4] As
Caxton prints it, with "my self" and "where in" each as two words, the
sentence contains one hundred and ten words. There are ten finite
verbs, expressed in fourteen words: took, read, remember, is
bounden, ought to put, is, had, was set, [was] written, thought; and
an additional had is implied in the elliptical clause. In form and usage,
each of these verbs is exactly as it would appear in twentieth century
English except that bounden retains an -*en* inflection for the past
participle which modern English has dropped (but compare modern
broken). In addition there are four verbals: two present participles,
having and following; one past participle, said; and an infinitive, to
eschew.

The sentence contains one independent clause, which has a
compound predicate and in which all three of the participles occur:
"then I, having no great charge of occupation, following the said
counsel, took a French book and read therein many strange and

marvellous histories." Everything in the sentence up to the beginning of this independent clause is an introductory adverbial clause, which itself contains three other subordinate clauses. The verb in the adverbial clause, remember, has two noun clauses as its direct objects: "that every man is bounden by the commandment & counsel of the wise man to eschew sloth and idleness" and "[that I] ought to put myself unto virtuous occupation and business." Except for the fact that the subject of *ought to put* is not expressed and cannot be inferred from the subject of *is bounden*, there is nothing in the syntax of this set of clauses which modern English could not tolerate. The nouns *sloth* and *idleness* occur as objects of the infinitive *to eschew*. They are modified by the adjective clause "which is mother and nourisher of vices." *Sloth* and *idleness* are doublets, as are *mother* and *nourisher*. Since *which* takes as its antecedent *sloth* and *idleness* and as its verb the singular *is*, the doublet is construed as singular — perhaps as logically on the basis of meaning as the modern English requirement that the two be taken as a plural on the basis of form.

After the independent clause, Caxton employs another group of subordinate clauses. The first requires some expansion of an elliptical construction if it is to be analyzed grammatically: "wherein I had of the same pleasure and delight as well for the novelty as [I had a degree of pleasure and delight] for the fair language of French." The *as well . . . as* contruction in modern English typically involves, however, the same sort of ellipsis.

Up to this point, little in Caxton's syntax creates a real problem; but the remaining two relative adjective clauses introduce the quality of Caxton's style which is a difficulty for the modern reader. The clause "which was in prose so well and compendiously set and written" begins with a relative pronoun for which we demand an antecedent. *Language* is a possibility grammatically, but it does not fully satisfy the sense of the sentence. *Book* is a remote antecedent; and *book* is coupled with *histories* in such a way as to make separating these two nouns, so that *which was* can agree with a singular antecedent, seem an exercise in false logic. The second of the relative adjective clauses, "which me thought I understood the sentence and substance of every matter," requires our supplying a preposition before *which*: *in which* or *of which*.

Caxton's English still employs some constructions such as this one which look back to a more fully inflected stage of the language when the case of the noun or pronoun would be shown in its form and no preposition would be needed. *Which* is not marked for case, and we are conscious of seeking for a preposition. Caxton's contemporaries probably supplied the necessary syntactical information without a thought, being accustomed to such constructions. This clause also contains an archaic expression, "me thought." Me is dative case, or what is now usually called the indirect object; thought is third person singular, with the subject unexpressed; the clause means "[it] seemed to me." The entire "which . . . I understood . . ." construction, like the "which was set and written . . ." clause, seems to modify book and histories.

As this discussion indicates, the sentence holds together, but it is burdened by clauses modifying clauses. Caxton can handle parallel structure, but he has difficulty with subordination. He was concerned, however, to get down the meaning, with all its many ramifications, not to parse his own syntax. If we look back for a moment at the vocabulary of the passages from *The Recuyell* which have been quoted, we find that *recuyell* itself is the single word which has entirely disappeared from modern usage and that only eschew and compendiously may be somewhat bookish to the modern ear. The significant difference between Caxton's English and ours lies in the use of phrases such as his "to put myself," "the said counsel," "as well for the novelty of the same." More than the broad syntactical pattern or the individual words in the vocabulary, the idioms or small set phrases distinguish Caxton's usage from our own.

The Recuyell Prologue is important in content as well as style, because what it says bears on the question of Caxton as translator and stylist. It will be profitable, therefore, to look further into it:

And for so much as this book was new and late made and drawn into French, and never had seen hit in our English tongue, I thought in myself hit should be a good business to translate hit into our English, to th'end that hit might be had as well in the realm of England as in other lands, and also for to pass therewith the time, and thus concluded in myself to being this said work. And forthwith took pen and ink and began boldly to run forth as blind Bayard [a traditional name for a horse] in this present work which is named *The Recuyell of the Trojan Historyes.*

And afterwards when I remembered myself of my simpleness and unperfectness that I had in both languages, that is, to wit, in French & in English, for in France was I never, and was born & learned mine English in Kent in the Weald, where I doubt not is spoken as broad and rude English as is in any place of England, & have continued by the space of .xxx. year for the most part in the countries of Brabant, Flanders, Holland, and Zeeland; and thus when all these things came to fore [before] me after that I had made and written a five or six quires, I fell in despair of this work and purposed no more to have continued therein and those quires laid apart, and in two year after labored no more in this work.

And was fully in will to have left hit, till on a time hit fortuned that the right high, excellent, and right virtuous princess, my right redoubted lady, my lady Margaret, by the grace of God, sister unto the king of England and of France, my sovereign lord, Duchess of Burgundy . . . sent for me to speak with her good grace of diverse matters, among the which I let her highness have knowledge of the foresaid beginning of this work, which anon commanded me to show the said .v. or .vi. quires to her said grace, and when she had seen them, anon she found a default in mine English, which she commanded me to amend and moreover commanded me straightly [directly] to continue and make an end of the residue then not translated, whose dreadful commandment I durst in no wise disobey because I am a servant unto her said grace and receive of her yearly fee and other many good and great benefits and also hope many more to receive of her highness; but forthwith went and labored in the said translation after my simple and poor cunning, also [exactly or entirely so] nigh [near, closely] as I can following mine author, meekly beseeching the bounteous highness of my said lady that of her benevolence [she] list [wish] to accept & take in gree [with favor] this simple & rude work here following; and if there be anything written or said to her pleasure, I shall think my labor well employed, and whereas there is default, that she arette [attribute] hit to the simpleness of my cunning [skill, knowledge, ability] which is full small in this behalf [in this respect; *The Oxford English Dictionary* cites Caxton's translation of *Feats of Arms*, 1489, for the idiom "in this behalf" in this sense] and require & pray all them that shall read this said work to correct hit & to hold me excused of the rude & simple translation. And thus I end my Prologue. (Crotch, pp. 4–5)

Although Caxton utilizes subordinate constructions, his clauses are chiefly linked together with ands: "And for so much," "And never had seen hit." He manages a complex array of parallel verb phrases: "thought in myself," "and thus concluded in myself," "and forthwith took pen and ink . . . ." The sentence rushes forward with an impetuosity which fits well to the sense of what Caxton is saying. The figure of blind Bayard is not new with Caxton, but it is graced here with perfect aptness.

The sentence beginning "And afterward when I remembered . . . ," leads him into such a long digression that he is forced to return to his starting point by a repetition—*"and thus when all these things came before me* after I had made and written a five or six quires, I fell in despair . . . ." If the capital letter at "And was fully in will" signals a new sentence, its subject, I, is implied but not stated. When he mentions Margaret, he must mention all her claims to renown. The helpful which enables him to recover himself and plunge on until he is forced to haul in another relative, whose, to supply him a new start, "whose dreadful commandment." But joins three verb phrases: "I *durst* in no wise *disobey* . . . *but* . . . *went* and *labored* . . . ," with a long clause intervening: "because I am servant . . . ." Having made his way intelligibly and even rather creditably through this thicket of ands and whichs, Caxton seems relieved to conclude simply and briefly: "And thus I end my Prologue."

The modern editor, by judicious punctuation and paragraphing, helps the reader through Caxton's plethora of clauses and phrases. Caxton's own light punctuation, however, suggests very clearly a world in which every matter related to his central idea stands out in his mind and in his syntax with great sharpness. He manages to force every fact into the foreground. He keeps his reader's attention focused on the desperate man striving to carry through to the end a job which is almost too much for him, and at the same time, he assures Margaret of Burgundy that she has his devoted and unflagging respect and attention. Cumbered as he is by a propensity to verbosity, by a language which has not yet fully shaped the grammar of its prose, and by the need to keep his patronness well in view, Caxton manages to tell us what he desires about his love of this book, his wish to be useful, and his frustration at a task which has become a chore. He is making the language work for him, but he must sometimes do so by main strength and awkwardness.

Two other matters must be touched upon before we leave *The Recuyell* Prologue. The occurrence of hit for it may surprise the unwary reader; but the form hit had good historical authority if we go back to Old English. *The Oxford English Dictionary* shows examples of hit from the *Old English Chronicle*, 878 A.D., through Queen Elizabeth I, 1586–1587. Hit has now sunk to a substandard dialect form, but only because of convention; there is nothing intrinsically inferior in hit, though it has passed from standard modern usage.

The protest Caxton makes of his own lack of skill and his propensity to error may be quite sincere, but it is also an example of a standard topos—a conventional formula which still occurs in that auctorial disclaimer in the typical preface, that friends have helped greatly by their suggestions but that errors are the responsibility of the humble author's own self. We need not assume, therefore, that Caxton was unduly diffident about his skill as a stylist.

In summary, *The Recuyell of the Historyes of Troye* has offered an opportunity to look at Caxton in three ways: As a stylist at the earliest point in his publishing career, he already demonstrated two marked tendencies—toward the clear, direct, simple statement and toward complex, indirect, and verbose construction. He sometimes drew upon a source for the sentence structure and vocabulary of his own prose; but at other times he constructed for himself the syntax which would convey his thought.

Reynard the Fox (first edition about 1481) falls midway of Caxton's career as a translator. In *The Recuyell*, he translated from French, for which he professed great admiration; his source for *Reynard the Fox* is Dutch, a language about which Caxton did not comment. Caxton's Epilogue insists that he has made a close translation, and a comparison of the Dutch and English texts bears him out. Since Dutch is allied to German and to English, even the reader who knows no Dutch may see the closeness of Caxton to his source in the quotations which follow.

Het was omtrent pinxteren also dattet wout dan gaerne lustelic gestelt plech te wesen. van loueren bloesseme bloemen wel rukende ende mede van voghelen ghesanghe

It was about the time of Pentecost or Whitsuntide that the woods commonly be lusty and gladsome, and the trees clad with leaves and blossoms and the ground with herbs and flowers sweet smelling, and also the fowls and birds sing melodiously in their harmony,

Alsoe dat dye edel coninck van allen dieren woude des pinxtere dages te stade een eerlic hof houden dat hi ouer al sijn lant te weten dede

that the lion, the noble king of all beasts, would in the holy days of this feast hold an open court at stade which he did to know over all in his land.[5]

Caxton cannot resist the impulse to expand, particularly through the doublet: fowls and birds. He has generally, as his Epilogue indicates, followed the source closely, even to the use of stade in a way which modern scholars and, we may suspect, Caxton, cannot explicate.

Caxton's translation of *Reynard the Fox* is the one for which he is most famous, for it remains in steady demand. He might have spoiled his own effort by an attempt to make the language fine or, to use Caxton's word, ornate. Some right instinct for style told him that these animals need a plain, straightforward style to set off their outrageous behavior.

Caxton's translation of the *Aeneid*, usually called *Eneydos*, was published almost at the end of his career [1490]. Although no special pleading can turn Caxton's unfortunate translation into a work of art, or even a workmanly job, the Prologue he wrote for *Eneydos* not only offers an example of his own late prose style but also contains his best-known story and indicates his love for language. The Prologue begins: "After diverse works made, translated, and achieved, having no work in hand, I, sitting in my study whereas lay many diverse pamphlets and books, happened that to my hand came a little book in French, which late was translated out of Latin by some noble clerk of France, which book is named *Eneydos*, made in Latin by that noble poet & great clerk Virgil, which book I saw over [looked over] and read therein . . ." (Crotch, p. 107).

This sentence contains much that is typical of Caxton's style: the multiplication of synonyms—made, translated, achieved—and the use of the subject I without a verb and of the verb happened without a subject expressed (or if we construe I as the subject of happened, then the verb with an improperly phrased object, "that to my hand came a little book in French") are constructions of a kind Caxton used throughout his career. The which clauses are strung together with more or less parallel structure but without intrinsic parallelism of thought: "which late was translated . . ."; "which book is named Eneydos . . ."; "which book I saw over and read therein. . . ."

Caxton then introduces his admiration for the language of the French text:

In which book I had great pleasure, by cause of the fair and honest terms & words in French, which I never saw to fore [before] like, nor none so pleasant nor so well ordered, which book as me seemed should be much requisite to noble men to see as well for the eloquence as the histories, how well [although] that many hundred years passed was the said book of *Eneydos* with other works made and learned daily in schools, specially in Italy & other places, which history the said Virgil made in meter. (Crotch, pp. 107–108)

We have in some respects returned to *The Recuyell* Prologue, for the account of how the old printer came upon *Eneydos* among the books and pamphlets in his study reminds us of his discovery of the other work. The description of "the fair and honest terms & words in

French" also reminds us of *The Recuyell* Prologue's "fair language of French." The "me seemed" construction is the same in syntax and meaning as *The Recuyell's* "me thought." He took "pleasure and delight" in *The Recuyell;* "great pleasure" in *Eneydos.* Even details— the choice of the phrase to fore or the use of said as a participial modifier—"the said counsel," "the said book"—are familiar.

Again, *The Recuyell* recounts the translator's difficulties and uncertainties in the pursuit of the translation; so does *Eneydos:*

And when I had advised me in this said book, I delibered [deliberated] and concluded to translate it into English, and forthwith took a pen & ink and wrote a leaf or twain, which I oversaw again to correct it. And when I saw the fair & strange terms therein, I doubted [feared] that it should not please some gentlemen which late blamed me, saying that in my translations I had over-curious terms which could not be understood of [by] common people, and desired me to use old and homely terms in my translations. And fain would I satisfy every man, and so to do took an old book and read therein; and certainly the English was so rude and broad that I could not well understand it. And also my lord abbot of Westminster did do show to me late certain evidences written in old English, for to reduce [bring] it into our English now used. And certainly it was written in such wise that it was more like to Dutch than English. I could not reduce nor bring it to be understonden.

And certainly our languge now used varieth far from that which was used and spoken when I was born. For we Englishmen been born under the domination of the moon, which is never steadfast, but every wavering, waxing one season and waneth & decreaseth another season. And that common English that is spoken in one shire varieth from another. In so much that in my days happened that certain merchants were in a ship in Thames for to have sailed over the sea into Zeeland, and for lack of wind they tarried at foreland [i.e., at a strip of land along the Thames—"land before something," such as a ridge—see *The Oxford English Dictionary*] and went to land for to refresh them. And one of them named Sheffield, a mercer, came into an house and axed [asked] for meat [food], and specially he axed after *eggs.* And the good wife answered that she could speak no French. And the merchant was angry, for he also could speak no French but would have had eggs, and she understood him not. And then at last another said that he would have *eyren.* Then the good wife said that she understood him well. Lo, what should a man in these days now write—*eggs* or *eyren.* Certainly it is hard to please every man by cause of diversity & change of language.

For in these days every man that is in any reputation in his country will utter his communication and matters in such manners & terms that few men shall understand them. And some honest and great clerks [scholars] have been with me and desired me to write the most curious terms that I could find. And thus between plain rude & curious I stand abashed. But in my judgment, the common terms that be daily used been lighter to be understood than the old and ancient English. And for as much as this present book is not for a rude, uplandish man to labor therein nor read it, but only for a clerk & a noble gentleman that feeleth and understandeth in [about] feats of arms, in love, & in noble chivalry, therefore in a mean between both I have reduced & translated this said book into our English, not over-rude nor curious but in such terms as shall be understanden, by God's grace, according to my copy. And if any man will entermete in [undertake] reading of hit and findeth such terms that he cannot understand, let him go read and learn Virgil or the *Epistles* of Ovid, and there he shall see and understand lightly all, if he have a good reader & informer. For this book is not for every rude and uncunning man to see, but to clerks and very [true] gentlemen that understand gentleness and science [learning; the concept of "the gentleman and scholar" is an old one]. (Crotch, pp. 108–09)

Caxton concludes the *Eneydos* Prologue with a statement about the author's limitations similar to that which appears in the Prologue to *The Recuyell of the Historyes of Troye*. He speaks at length of the learning and skill of "Master John Skelton, late created poet laureate at the University of Oxford," who is charged to correct and explain the text, for "I suppose he hath drunken of Helicon's well" (Crotch, p. 109). These comments about Skelton suggest that Caxton is more annoyed than enamored with Skelton's views of how Caxton should write, but Skelton may have been one of the gentlemen who undertook to instruct Caxton in the technique of composition. Caxton dedicates his book to Prince Arthur, son of Henry VII, and so ends his last and most famous Prologue.

Perhaps in one conspicuous way only does the style of this last Prologue differ from that of the first: it relies much more heavily on a series of independent clauses linked by ands than upon the which constructions that mark *The Recuyell* Prologue. In content, the writer indicates more confidence in his own ability and more assurance that he can complete the task which he has set for himself. But there is the same personal note, the same technique of drawing every matter into the foreground, the same implication that matters are being set down as they come to mind with no great degree of revision or artful design which we feel in reading the Prologue to *The Recuyell*.

Caxton's style, in fact, seems to vary more with the occasion and subject than as a result of the writer's experience and development. In translating *Reynard the Fox*, Caxton models his sentence patterns on the homely style of the Dutch, which precisely suits the animal fable.

In explaining his translation of a classic, he elevates his style to fit the subject. In dedicating his work to a noble patron, he strives for an ornateness to match the occasion. That this is true, from the beginning to the end of Caxton's career, can be demonstrated by recalling the comments about Margaret of Burgundy quoted earlier in this chapter and comparing them to the Epilogue to *Fifteen Oes*, perhaps the last thing Caxton composed independently and set in print: "These prayers tofore written been enprinted by the commandments of the most high & virtuous princess, our liege lady Elizabeth by the grace of God Queen of England & of France & also of the right high & most noble princess Margaret, mother unto our sovereign lord the king, &c" (Crotch, p. 111).

Evidence of Caxton's vocabulary is to be seen throughout the quotations from his work, both in this chapter and in preceding ones. The conclusion is, as we have noted, obvious: Much of Caxton's vocabulary remains active in modern English. His most marked contribution is of words formed on the model of words in the source he is translating, and of these a substantial part have disappeared from current use.

II *Caxton's Comments about His Own Translations*

Translation may range from free to faithful. Caxton's are often simple word for word renderings, but he sometimes is freer, and he often adds observations of his own to the text that he is translating. Caxton's prologues may note the method by which he is translating. In the Prologue to *The Recuyell of the Historyes of Troye*, he says that he has been literal, as "nigh as I can following mine author" (Crotch, p. 5). In the Prologue to *Jason* he declares his intention of "following mine author as nigh as I can" (Crotch, p. 33) without changing, adding, or deleting. In the Prologue to *The Mirror of the World* he proposes "to follow as nigh as God will give me grace . . ." (Crotch, p. 54), and in the Epilogue to *The Mirror* asserts that he has done all he can to make "it so plain that every man reasonable may understand it . . ." (Crotch, p. 58). In the Epilogue to *Reynard the Fox* and the Prologue to *The Royal Book*, he vows an intention of fidelity to the source. *Feats of Arms* aims at clarity, so that it may be "understandable to every man," but Caxton affirms that it will "not much vary" (Crotch, p. 104) from his source. In the Prologue to *Blanchardin and Eglantine*, Caxton apologizes for the "rude and common English" because he does not know "the art of rhetoric nor of such gay terms as now be said in these days and used." If he is understood, however, "that shall suffice" (Crotch, p. 105). *Four Sons of Aymon* is announced as "rude" and "simple" but faithful (Crotch, p. 106).

Such fidelity does not produce greatness for Caxton. Chaucer turned Boccaccio's *Teseida* into *The Knight's Tale* and his *Filostrato* into *Troilus and Criseyde*. We do not hesitate to call these Chaucer's creative works, any more than we hesitate to recognize Shakespeare's *Troilus and Cressida* as his own or to accept the Fletcher and Shakespeare—if Shakespeare's it is—*Two Noble Kinsmen* as a creative work, though it derives directly from *The Knight's Tale* and is, furthermore, signally inferior to it. Shakespeare's *Troilus* is a particularly interesting case in point, because his sources are generally said to include the strong influence of Caxton's translation of Lefèvre's *Recuyell of the Historyes of Troye*.

Caxton's translations do not achieve Chaucer's or Shakespeare's transformation of old matter into new; but they served as a fifteenth century bridge between the flowering of the English Middle Ages in the fourteenth century and the Renaissance. The taste which read long prose tales of Troy, sustained by the pious belief that they recorded the history of one's ancestors, is no longer with us, but a line of continuity exists: Shakespeare read Caxton's *Recuyell;* we read Shakespeare.

If some of Caxton's contemporaries—as he remarks in the Prologue to *Eneydos*—complained about his translations, some of them also requested these translations. Margaret of Burgundy, at the outset of Caxton's publishing career, corrected his text of *The Recuyell* and ordered him to complete it. Hugh Bryce commissioned *The Mirror of the World. The Golden Legend* was completed with the encouragement of the Earl of Arundel; and the Prologue to *The Golden Legend* lists as works Englished "at the request of certain lords, ladies, and gentlemen" (Crotch, p. 71): *The Recuyell, The Game and Play of the Chess, Jason, The Mirror of the World, Ovid's Metamorphoses,* and *Godfrey of Boloyne.* Some esquire asked Caxton to translate *The Order of Chivalry,* and a lady requested *The Knight of the Tower.* William Daubeney asked for the translation of *Charles the Great,* and William Praat for *The Book of Good Manners.* An unnamed merchant asked for *The Royal Book;* Henry VII for *Feats of Arms;* and his mother, Margaret, for *Blanchardin and Eglantine.* For John, Earl of Oxford, Caxton translated *Four Sons of Aymon* and a now lost life of Robert, Earl of Oxford. Caxton had a reputation as a translator sufficient to bring Earl Rivers to him with a translation of *The Dicts or*

Sayings of the Philosophers, which the earl wished Caxton to correct.

Someone else would have brought a press into England if Caxton had not; but, as many of Caxton's biographers note, it is doubtful that anyone else would have brought the same zeal, judgment, and ability for supplying translations suited for English readers.

CHAPTER 8

Caxton's Contribution to English Letters: An Assessment

I An Overview of Caxton's Literary Theory and Practice

CAXTON'S demonstration, through what he wrote and printed, of his sense of values provides a means for arriving at a statement of his literary theory. Caxton was, first, a moralist and a critic who considered books to be instruments of instruction. For Caxton and his age, history was a series of lessons which would enable the human race to find the clue to civilization and to right action. Such volumes as *Polychronicon, The Game and Play of the Chess, Caton, Cordial,* and *The Royal Book* bear witness to Caxton's belief that books must teach and that their principal message should concern the salvation of the soul. Nonetheless, Caxton's Medieval otherworldliness is constantly balanced against his involvement with the temporal world. He extracted the material in *The Description of Britain* and printed it because "the nobleness and worthiness" of Britain (Crotch, p. 40) were insufficiently known, and he recommended the essays of Cicero for what they teach about adapting to the situations of mortal life.

Caxton had a strong feeling for fact and for an authoritative source. He insists, for example, that *The Book of Good Manners* rests on the authority of the Bible and upon the words of "holy saints, doctors [learned men], philosophers, and poets" (Crotch, p. 100), but he also knew that literature need not be factual or authoritative to be instructive. The Epilogue to the first edition of *Reynard the Fox,* identified by Blake as a translation from the Dutch,[1] insists that the reader "may find therein many a good wisdom and learnings, by which he may come to virtue and worship" (Crotch, p. 62). Indeed, the written text was to Caxton a means of preserving wisdom. In the Prologue to *The Mirror of the*

130

World (in part translated), Caxton declares oral language to be "perishing, vain, and forgettable," whereas "writings dwell & abide permanently. . . ." From antiquity men have prepared written records "to the end that science and arts learned and founded of things passed might be had in perpetual memory and remembrance"[2] for the enhancement of wisdom.

Evidence that Caxton also possessed a sense of humor is scattered through his work. We have noticed Caxton's addition to the *Fables of Aesop* of the humorous story of the widow's determination to accept a new husband. His Epilogue to *The Dicts or Sayings of the Philosophers* contains a somewhat clumsy stretch of jesting with Rivers about his omission of Socrates' strictures against women. Caxton then adds the Socratic sayings, of which the following is a typical example: Socrates "saw a woman that bare [carried] fire, of whom he said that the hotter bare the colder."[3]

Caxton liked to round out the treatment of a topic. One reason he gives for printing Lefèvre's *Jason* is that it supplements *The Recuyell of the Historyes of Troye;* and adding Charles the Great to Arthur and Godfrey completed his treatment of the Christian worthies. However, Caxton also appreciated literature for its purely esthetic values. Even in so pedestrian a work as *The Recuyell,* Caxton was attracted by the language. He recognized rhetoric as being so powerful as to entail dangers if falsely used, as he evidences in the Proem to *Polychronicon.* He sets Chaucer above "all other writers in our English" (Crotch, p. 69) for the excellence of his style as well as for his wisdom.

If we ask what Caxton valued in books, one answer is certainly a lesson. Another is fine language. But another of which we must not lose sight is this: he loved a good story. Although we do not know the capacity in which Caxton entered the service of Margaret of Burgundy, the first time we hear of his relationship with her, he is showing her a story, *The Recuyell of the Historyes of Troye.* When we consider Chaucer, Gower, Lydgate, and Malory, we recognize with Caxton that what these four have in common is that they work in the medium of the story. When he chose something to translate, it was often a story: *The Recuyell, Jason, Metamorphoses, Reynard the Fox,* the *Fables of Aesop, Charles the Great, Paris and Vienne, Blanchardin and Eglantine, Eneydos, Four Sons of Aymon.* When Caxton has something to tell, he is likely to tell it through a story—a true story about how he translated and printed *The Recuyell,* a story about some travelers who set out for Zeeland and discovered the instability of the

English language. Caxton did not theorize extensively about the function of the story, but his translations, his choices of books, and his own stories show that he recognized a story as a primary means of achieving the principal end of literary composition—the reduction of experienced diversity to a unified and comprehensible totality.

Caxton was not a thinker in advance of his times: he did not publish religious materials designed to produce the Reformation; his histories were in the old chronicle tradition; and his scientific works were few in number and traditional in content. Columbus could not have derived much information from *The Mirror of the World* or Higden's *Polychronicon;* and in the year following Caxton's death, Columbus discovered a New World on the side of the globe which Higden had declared to be all water.

Caxton's books reflect the scope of his world. He printed a substantial though by no means definitive body of the then available great English literature, and he provided translations of both recent and ancient books from many countries and centuries. His choices reflect the fact that he belonged to two worlds socially. As a merchant, he moved in the world of trade; but as a merchant venturer, he was a member of a group whose power extended into government circles. As we have noted, Caxton showed no real concern for what the plowboy might read; he published what he felt the upper and middle classes required. He was apparently a thoroughly orthodox and devout churchman, but his press was far from sectarian. However much the early press depended upon patrons, Caxton was able to give it a substantial degree of independence and to deliver it from the narrow range that is suggested by surviving library catalogues and by other lists of Medieval manuscripts. Caxton was in touch with the life of his contemporaries; he never drew away into printing the esoteric and remote.

Caxton's books suggest the end of much that is Medieval. To the Middle Ages, the curious animals of the bestiary tradition are a means of stating theological positions through allegory; at the end of the fifteenth century they are merely curious animals. The old stratification of society into three estates—aristocracy, clergy, and peasantry—has expanded to accommodate the merchant class. Caxton printed *Feats of Arms* for the first of the Tudor rulers who would lead England into a new role in the world, but neither Caxton nor Henry VII seemed to sense that the chivalric age was, in practicality, past. But while Caxton desired to hold to old values, he was aware of new technological means for forwarding his end. It was, after all, Caxton who went to Cologne, learned to print, and came to Westminster to operate England's first press.

Whether Caxton is admired as a prose stylist is a matter of taste, but there is general agreement that in his translations, he is not uniformly effective. Even so, he manages to make his material intelligible, despite the fact that his syntax may be a puzzle or his vocabulary overladen with synonyms. Caxton wrote a small body of essays which constitute his prologues and epilogues. Those which deal with literary criticism, such as the ones prepared for the various editions of Chaucer, stand out in a vast sea of critical writing for their clarity, charm, and illumination. The personal essays, such as the prologues to *The Recuyell of the Historyes of Troye* and to *Eneydos*, introduce a writer whom we are glad to know as a person. Caxton's place as an author, as separate from his place as a printer and editor, is small; but it is secure.

Wynkyn de Worde records Caxton's death in the colophon of the edition which he printed of Caxton's translation of the *Lives of the Fathers*, with the Latin title *Vitas patrum:* "Thus endeth the most virtuous history of the devout and right renowned lives of holy fathers living in desert, worthy of remembrance to all well-disposed persons, which hath been translated out of French into English by William Caxton of Westminster, late dead, and finished at the last day of his life."[4] That Caxton died a translator constitutes poetic justice, for his work was not so much creation as transmission. Caxton created neither the printing press nor much of the material that he printed—but he put into accessible form a representative body of late Medieval literature; and he left in his printed books the evidence that, while the Renaissance would produce more writers, more genres, more total volumes than the Middle Ages, it would not produce better work than that of the one Medieval writer whom Caxton recognized as different in degree and kind from all his peers—plump, jesting, sometimes bawdy, but ultimately and eloquently moral and sage old Geoffrey Chaucer. It is no mean accomplishment for Caxton to have recognized the cleverest invention of his era and to have used that invention to publish its finest poet.

E. Gordon Duff, in *Fifteenth Century English Books: A Bibliography of Books and Documents Printed in England and of Books for the English Market Printed Abroad*, lists 431 items. Pollard and Redgrave, in *A Short-Title Catalogue of Books Printed in England, Scotland, & Ireland, and of English Books Printed Abroad 1475–*

1640, include 26,143 items. The numbers speak clearly of the multiplication of printed materials in the one hundred and forty years after the close of the incunabulum period. Multiplication of literary genres is less dramatic than the multiplication in sheer numbers of volumes, but literary forms quite obviously changed shape as the Medieval world gave way to the Renaissance. The Middle Ages, for example, produced epic poetry; but the epic becomes a new if not a better thing in the era bounded by the *Faerie Queene* (1590) and *Paradise Lost* (1667). Although Caxton printed no plays, the Medieval world also had its drama; but the Renaissance exploded with an array of dramatic forms for which Shakespeare's Polonius can scarcely find sufficient labels: "tragedy, comedy, history, pastoral, pastoral-comical, historical-pastoral, tragical-historical, tragical-comical-historical-pastoral, scene individable, or poem unlimited: Seneca cannot be too heavy, nor Plautus too light."[5] Polonius's reference to Seneca and Plautus gives a clue to the reason for the change: English poetry and drama in the Renaissance began to draw upon Classical models in a way that the Middle Ages had not.

The Medieval lyric, either as a self-contained unit or embedded in a narrative poem, achieves both beauty and depth, but the sonnet, the pastoral, the metaphysical lyric, are Renaissance manifestations. Yet the Renaissance grows from the Middle Ages: Behind much of Shakespeare lies the Medieval chronicle history; even Falstaff has Medieval precursors in the vice of the morality plays. Behind *Paradise Lost* lies the Corpus Christi drama, the bestiary tradition, and much else in Medieval religious thought. So, too, a metaphysical lyric like John Donne's "Busy old fool, unruly sun" echoes Troilus's great aubade, "O Fool [Titan, the sun], well may men thee despise. . . ."[6]

II   *Caxton's Publications Compared with Those of Other Printers*

A comparison of Caxton's titles with those of other printers in the fifteenth, sixteenth, and early seventeenth centuries reveals much about the place of Caxton's work in English cultural and social history.[7] One fact which emerges from an examination of the titles of English incunabula is that in the fifteenth century, Caxton was almost the sole supplier of narrative poetry, prose narratives, fables, histories, courtesy books, and scientific pieces in a market that was dominated by grammars, missals, yearbooks, and statutes. The output of Caxton's press suffers by comparison with that of others on one score only, its dearth of solid philosophical material; for *Boethius de consolatione philosophiae* is the solitary philosophical work of real significance which Caxton printed, though several other of his publications were popular philosophical pieces. Plays and lyric poetry are poorly represented among fifteenth century books that come from all English presses.

Little of what Caxton printed was published by any other English printer or for the English trade by a foreign printer before 1491, the year of Caxton's death. In competition with Caxton's editions, readers had a choice of a volume of *Chronicles* issued by William de Machlinia or one by the St. Albans printer, of *Horae* from Machlinia or from a Paris printer, of Machlinia's *Festum transfigurationis Iesu Christi*, Colard Mansion's *Troyes* and *Jason* in French (*Troyes* and *Jason* are sometimes, however, attributed to Caxton), Gerard Leeu's *Directorium sacerdotum*, Theodoric Rood and Thomas Hunte's *Festial*, Michael Wenssler's *Missale*, the St. Albans *Rhetorica*, and Richard Pynson's *Canterbury Tales*.[8] Even if we make a conservative attribution to Caxton and count the Bruges *Troyes* and *Jason* in French as Mansion's, not Caxton's, only a little more than forty-three percent of Caxton's titles, excluding the indulgences, achieved publication by others between his death and the close of the century. No formal copyright existed, and such things as church service books may have been regarded as common property, but it was obviously not the practice to pirate, perhaps because piracy would have produced a glutted market. The later reappearance of Caxton titles occurred very often from the press of Wynkyn de Worde, Caxton's successor, which suggests that these publications were marketable.

Following Caxton's titles into the sixteenth and early seventeenth centuries reveals that they had varying fates. Some of his religious texts which proved popular include John Mirk's *Festial*, usually published with *Four Sermons*, which runs to twelve fifteenth century entries in the *Short-Title Catalogue*, seven between 1502 and 1532, but none thereafter. The *Speculum vitae Christi* or *The Mirror of the Life of Christ* is given four fifteenth century entries, including two by Caxton; six in the sixteenth century; and one in 1620. *The Golden Legend*, printed twice by Caxton, is entered a total of eight times through 1527. *Fifteen Oes* reappeared once, in 1529. The printing history of Caxton's religious texts, as this sample shows, suggests that for about forty years after his death many of these works remained in demand, but that the market changed rapidly after that, not so much because fewer religious books were wanted perhaps as because different works were in demand subsequent to the development of Reformation ideas. In the Classics, the authors Caxton chose— Cicero, Ovid, Virgil—experienced continuous and accelerated popularity, with the addition of great numbers of new titles. Texts of the Classics became much more widely available to both printer and reader in the sixteenth century. *Aesop* was often reprinted.

Of Caxton's romances, *Le Morte d'Arthur* reappeared in two editions from de Worde's press, and then in [1557], [1585?], and 1634 from other presses. *Charles the Great* and *Godfrey of Boloyne* were not reprinted, but *Four Sons of Aymon* made four reappearances. Only Gerard Leeu, in Antwerp, tried his luck with Lefèvre's *Jason*, but *The Recuyell of the Historyes of Troye* is entered in the *Short-Title Catalogue* four times in the sixteenth century and three times in the seventeenth before 1640. Leeu also printed *Paris and Vienne* in 1492, as did de Worde and Pynson, probably both in 1510; and another compilation of the story received two early seventeenth century editions. The tedious tale of *Blanchardin and Eglantine* reappeared in 1595 and 1597.

The *Short-Title Catalogue* gives Chaucer's collected works fourteen entries between 1532 and 1640, but it has only five earlier entries under *The Canterbury Tales*—two of them Caxton's. *Troilus and Criseyde* waited from 1482 to 1517, but it then appeared again in [1526?] and in 1635.[9] *The Book of Fame* reappeared once; *The Parliament of Fowls,* twice. Gower's *Confessio amantis* was published by Thomas Berthelet in 1532 and in 1554. Lydgate's works had staggering popularity, and a great number of Lydgate titles, in addition to those printed by Caxton, appeared in the sixteenth and seventeenth centuries. The anonymous *Reynard the Fox* received two editions by Caxton, one by Pynson in the fifteenth century, and six more by 1640.

Instructional texts such as the *Donatus*, the *Rhetorica*, and the *Vocabulary in French and English* represent books which were popular as a kind but not as individual titles. *The Mirror of the World* was published once more [1529?], and the histories fared similarly: two volumes of the *Chronicles* appeared from presses other than Caxton's in the fifteenth century but not again, though chronicles of various kinds were popular. De Worde published the *Description of Britain* in 1498. Both de Worde and Peter Treveris published *Polychronicon*, in 1495 and 1527, respectively.

Caxton was, in general, fortunate though not infallible in choosing books that continued to demand publication. His press seems to have served the purpose for which he established it: to make readable books widely available.

III *Epilogue*

In *The Book of Fame*, a great golden eagle swoops down to carry the astonished Chaucer through the upper spheres into the houses of fame and rumor. Although the eagle is a messenger of Jupiter, sent to reward the poet for his diligent labors by a spectacular vision, the eagle is also a garrulous pedant who insists upon explaining the structure of the universe, the nature of the Milky Way, the theory of sound, and other matters, factual and fictional. In certain ways, the eagle is an apt metaphor for Caxton and his work; for Caxton used the press to open an entire new vision of the universe to the astonished Medieval reader, to batter him with information, to shove him into new experiences, and to teach him much that is true and more that is only report and rumor—but with all his limitations, or even because of his limitations, thoroughly human, thoroughly lovable, thoroughly delightful.

If we pursue this metaphor of the eagle's coming as Jupiter's messenger, we would certainly witness Caxton's acceptance of himself as an agent of the message that man must think not merely of this world but of the next—of death, judgment, heaven, and hell; for all the words that Caxton printed ultimately direct his readers to those four last words. He could add a naughty story about an amorous widow to a volume of idle tales called the *Fables of Aesop;* but his final story in that collection begins: "Now then I will finish all these fables with this tale that followeth, which a worshipful priest and a parson told me late." Caxton then tells of two masters of arts at Oxford who became respectively a rich dean and a poor, simple priest. When the dean "came riding into a good parish with a x or xii horse like a prelate and came into the church of this said parish and found there this good simple man, sometime his fellow," the dean asks the priest how much his benefice is worth. The priest replies: " 'If I do my true diligence in the cure of my parishioners in preaching and teaching and do my part longing [belonging] to my cure, I shall have heaven therefore.' " And, says Caxton, "This was a good answer . . ." (Crotch, pp. 88–89).

Notes and References

Chapter One

1. F. Gordon Duff, *Fifteenth Century English Books* (London, 1917; rpt. Meisenheim, Ger., 1964), lists ninety-six items as Caxton's and two as printed for him by William Maynyal. To these must be added the indulgence discovered in 1928 and possibly the *Image of Pity* prints. N. F. Blake, *Caxton and his World* (Elmsford, N.Y., 1969), Item 37, p. 229, adds *Epitoma sive isagogicum margarite castigate eloquentie*, discovered by Mrs. Jean E. Mortimer, and other titles to a total of one hundred and three. Christopher A. Webb, "Caxton's *Quattuor Sermones*. A Newly Discovered Edition," in D. E. Rhodes, ed., *Essays in Honour of Victor Scholderer* (Mainz, 1970), pp. 407–25, adds an edition. George D. Painter, *William Caxton: A Quincentenary Biography of England's First Printer* (London, 1976), p. 186, records his discovery of two additional *Horae*.

See also A[lfred] W. Pollard and G. R. Redgrave, *A Short-Title Catalogue of Books Printed in England, Scotland, & Ireland, and of English Books Printed Abroad, 1475–1640* (London, 1946), with *An Index of Printers* compiled by Paul G. Morrison (Charlottesville, Va., and London, 1950, 1961); Seymour de Ricci, *A Census of Caxtons*, Bibliographical Society, Illustrated Monographs, XV (London, 1909); George Watson, ed., *The New Cambridge Bibliography of English Literature*, I (Cambridge, 1974), columns 667–70; Robert H. Wilson, "Malory and Caxton," in *A Manual of the Writings in Middle English 1050–1500*, gen. ed., Albert E. Hartung, III (New Haven, 1972), 771–807, 924–51.

2. See E. F. Jacob, *The Fifteenth Century, 1399–1485*, The Oxford History of England, VI (Oxford, 1961), for a full historical account.

3. Ranulf Higden, *Polychronicon*, trans. John Trevisa, with Book 8 added by William Caxton (Westminster, [1482],) book 8, ch. 9, folios CCCCi, r-v-CCCCii, r; University Microfilms, Reel 13, from British Museum, Reference Number G. 6011-12. Higden is hereafter cited parenthetically within my text to this microfilm copy.

4. William Shakespeare, *Henry V*, Act II, Prologue, l. 6, in Hardin Craig, ed. *The Complete Works of Shakespeare* (Atlanta, 1951), p. 743.

5. William Caxton, Prologue, Raoul Lefèvre, *The Recuyell of the Historyes of Troye* (Bruges, 1475). Caxton's prologues and epilogues are reprinted in W. J. B[lyth] Crotch, ed., *The Prologues and Epilogues of William Caxton*, Early English Text Society, Original Series, CLXXVI (London, 1928; rpt. 1956); also in Nellie Slayton Aurner, *Caxton, Mirror of*

Fifteenth-Century Letters: A Study of the Literature of the First English Press (Boston and New York, 1926); and N. F. Blake, ed., *Caxton's Own Prose* (London, 1973). William Blades, *The Biography and Typography of William Caxton, England's First Printer*, 2nd rev. ed. (London and Strassburg, 1882), provides extensive excerpts from Caxton and also numerous facsimiles. Unless otherwise noted, my references to Caxton's prologues and epilogues are to Crotch's edition but with my own modernizations and are cited parenthetically.

6. See, for example, "Edward V," *Webster's Biographical Dictionary*, 1st ed. (Springfield, Mass., 1963), p. 468.

7. Thomas Hobbes, *Leviathan* (London, 1651), Pt. 1, ch. xiii.

8. See the bibliography for books which treat fully what is known and for articles on special problems. Four recent books which reevaluate data and report new findings are Painter; N. F. Blake, *Caxton and his World;* N. F. Blake, *Caxton: England's First Publisher* (London, 1976); and Richard Deacon, *A Biography of William Caxton, The First English Editor, Printer, Merchant, and Translator* (London, 1976). Crotch offers a valuable, detailed biographical introduction and reprints essential documents. An important early study, often in need of correction, is Blades.

9. Painter, pp. 8–10.

10. *The Book of Courtesy* [Westminster, 1477–1478]. A modern edition is: Frederick J. Furnivall, ed., *Caxton's Book of Curtesye, Printed at Westminster about 1477–8 A.D.*, Early English Text Society, Extra Series III (London, 1868, rpt. 1882, 1898); see pp. 33 and 41 for the lines quoted.

11. Crotch, pp. xlvii–lxv, discusses the merchant adventurers and the role of the governor of the English nation.

12. Painter, p. 44. See Painter, pp. 32-50, on the whole question of Caxton and the governorship.

13. [J. G. Birch? Alfred W. Pollard?], "William Caxton's Stay at Cologne," *Library: Transactions of the Bibliographical Society*, 4th Series, IV (1923), 50–52; Painter, pp. 48—58; Crotch, pp. lxxxiv–vii.

14. See Douglas C. McMurthrie, *The Book: The Story of Printing & Bookmaking*, 7th ed. (London, etc., 1943); Curt F. Bühler, *The Fifteenth Century Book* (Philadelphia and London, 1960); George Parker Winship, *Gutenberg to Plantin: An Outline of the Early History of Printing* (Cambridge, Mass., and London, 1926); Lawrence C. Wroth, ed., *A History of the Printed Book, Being the Third Number of "The Dolphin"* (New York, 1938); Victor Scholderer, *Johann Gutenberg, The Inventor of Printing* (London, 1963); Ronald B. McKerrow, *An Introduction to Bibliography for Literary Students* (Oxford, 1927); Arundell Esdaile, *A Student's Manual of Bibliography*, rev. by Roy Stokes (London, 1954); Fredson Bowers, *Principles of Bibliographical Description* (Princeton, N.J., 1949).

15. Michael Maittaire, *Annales Typographici*, I (The Hague, 1719), 27–30, reprints from Atkyns; Conyers Middleton, "A Dissertation Concern-

ing the Origin of Printing in England," *The Miscellaneous Works of the late Reverend and Learned Conyers Middleton, D.D.*, III (London, 1752), 229–54. See also E. Gordon Duff, *The Printers, Stationers and Bookbinders of Westminster and London from 1476 to 1535* (Cambridge, 1906), pp. 1–3; Deacon, pp. 88—91.

16. On the device, see Blades, pp. 138–40; William Blades, "Caxton's Device," *The Athenaeum*, 2689 (May 10, 1879), 601; E. Gordon Duff, *William Caxton* (Chicago, 1905), pp. 70–71; Henry R. Plomer, *William Caxton* (London and Boston, 1925), p. 151; John Clyde Oswald, *A History of Printing* (New York and London, 1928), p. 198; Painter, pp. 160–61.

17. Painter, p. 215.

18. Blades, *Biography and Typography*, p. 83; L. A. Sheppard, "A New Light on Caxton and Colard Mansion," *Signature*, New Series, XV (1952), 28–39; Painter, p. 61.

19. Watson, columns 667–68; Painter, p. 211; Duff, *Fifteenth Century English Books*, especially p. 125.

20. See George Parker Winship, *Printing in the Fifteenth Century* (Philadelphia and London, 1940), p. 145; Susan Cunnington, *The Story of William Caxton* (London, 1917), pp. 76–77; Blake, *Caxton and his World*, p. 61; Painter, pp. 59–71.

21. Painter, p. 65.

22. Painter, pp. 82–107, surveys the evidence concerning Caxton's removal to and establishment at Westminster.

23. A[lfred] W. Pollard, "The New Caxton Indulgence," *Library. Transactions of the Bibliographical Society*, 4th Series, IX (1928), 86–89; K. Povey, "The Caxton Indulgence of 1476," *Library*, 4th Series, XIX (1939), 462–64; Painter, pp. 80–85.

24. Painter, pp. 80–85, 211, and *passim*.

25. The *Advertisement* is often reprinted. See, for example, Blades, *Biography and Typography*, p. [239]; Duff, *Fifteenth Century English Books*, Item 80.

26. Plomer, p. 83.

27. Blades, *Biography and Typography*, p. 297.

28. Aurner, pp. 189–90; Blake, *Caxton and his World*, p. 93 and *passim*.

29. Winship, *Printing in the Fifteenth Century*, pp. 149–50.

30. This is a topic on which many scholars have speculated. For representative examples of the positions summarized in this and the immediately following paragraphs, see Blades, *Biography and Typography*, p. 339; Blake, *Caxton: England's First Publisher*, pp. 44–54, 192; Blake, *Caxton and his World*, *passim*; Painter, p. 173 and *passim*; Plomer, pp. 61–62, 83, 143–44; Winship, *Printing in the Fifteenth Century*, pp. 146–47; Curt F. Bühler, *William Caxton and His Critics* (Syracuse, N.Y., 1960), pp. 13–14; Aurner, pp. 189–90; Donald B. Sands, "Caxton as a Literary Critic," *Papers of the Bibliographical Society of America*, LI (1957), 316–18; Karl Julius

Holzkneckt, *Literary Patronage in the Middle Ages* (New York, 1966), pp. 114–15.

31. Aurner, p. 184; Bühler, *The Fifteenth Century Book*, p. 135n; Crotch, p. xlvi; Blake, *Caxton: England's First Publisher*, pp. 34–40; Blake, *Caxton and his World*, pp. 35–45.

32. See the indexes to *The [London] Times, The Times Literary Supplement*, and *The New York Times* for various stories concerning Caxton's Ovid. See also A.N.L. Munby, "The Case of the 'Caxton' Manuscript of Ovid: Reflections on the Legislation Controlling the Export of Works of Art from Great Britain," *The Flow of Books and Manuscripts: Papers Read at the Clark Library Seminar, March 30, 1968*, ed. A. N. L. Munby and Lawrence W. Towner, with a Foreword by James Thorpe (Los Angeles, 1969), pp. 3–31.

Chapter Two

1. See Figures 25 and 26 in *Caxton's Mirrour of the World*, ed. Oliver H. Prior, Early English Text Society, Extra Series, CX (London and New York), 1913 (for 1912).

2. See Duff, *Fifteenth Century English Books*, Items 39–40. Crotch, p. lxxxvii, reprints de Worde's lines.

3. See Albert C. Baugh, ed., *A Literary History of England*, 2nd ed. (New York, 1967), pp. 150, 268; A.C. Crombie, *Medieval and Early Modern Science*, 2nd ed., II (Garden City, N. Y., 1959), 112; Edward Grant, ed., *A Source Book in Medieval Science* (Cambridge, Mass., 1974), p. 813; Lynn Thorndike, *A History of Magic and Experimental Science during the First Thirteen Centuries of Our Era*, II (New York, 1923; 5th rpt. 1958), 405–406; John Edwin Wells, *A Manual of the Writings in Middle English 1050–1400* (New Haven, 1926), p. 438.

4. See Wilson, p. 783.

5. Prior, pp. 7–8; further quotations from *The Mirror of the World* are based on the Prior edition and are documented in parentheses in the text.

6. See *The Compact Edition of The Oxford English Dictionary*, 2 vols, (Oxford, 1971) for this and all further citations from *The Oxford English Dictionary*.

7. John Milton, "Lycidas," ll. 114–117, reprinted in *The Complete Poetical Works of John Milton*, ed. Douglas Bush (Boston, 1965), p. 145.

8. Prior, p. 101, n.3.

9. John Milton, *Paradise Lost*, Book I, ll. 192–97, 200–10, reprinted in Bush, pp. 216–17.

10. T. H. White, ed. and trans., *The Bestiary: A Book of Beasts, Being a Translation from a Latin Bestiary of the Twelfth Century* (New York, 1954; Capricorn ed., 1960), p. 8.

11. On authorship, see Blades, *Biography and Typography*, pp. 203–204. and Wayland Johnson Chase, ed. and tr., *The Distichs of Cato, A Famous*

Medieval Textbook, University of Wisconsin Studies in the Social Sciences and History, No. 7 (Madison, 1922), pp. 1–3; on popularity, Chase, pp. 4–8. In the *British Museum, General Catalogue of Printed Books, Photolithographic Edition to 1955* (London, 1965), XXXV, the entries for this title occupy almost seventeen columns.

12. Clarissa P. Farrar and Austin P. Evans, *Bibliography of English Translations from Medieval Sources* (New York, 1946), Item 2816, identifies the French translator as Guillaume de Tignonville and the original compilation as Arabic. The Rivers Prologue can be found in the three texts reproduced by University Microfilms, Shipment 1, Reel 4, from copies in the British Museum, the second and third identified as Reference Numbers C. 10. 6. 2. and I. B. 55143; the Prologue begins on leaf 2 in each copy. See also the facsimile by William Blades (London, 1877).

13. William Blades, ed., *Morale Proverbes* (London, 1859), reproduces the full text in facsimile. See leaves 1, and 4, for the lines quoted.

14. In addition to the microfilm copy, see the edition "Caxton: Tulle of Olde Age," ed. Heinz Susebach, *Textuntersuchung mit Literarischer Einführung, Studien zur Englischen Philologie*, LXXV (Halle, 1933), 32–33, 85.

Chapter Three

1. Painter, p. 12. See also Wilson, p. 776.

2. See Domenico Comparetti, *Vergil in the Middle Ages*, tr. E. F. M. Benecke (New York, rpt. 1929), and John Webster Spargo, *Virgil the Necromancer*, Harvard Studies in Comparative Literature, X (Cambridge, Mass., 1934), on the curious Medieval reputation of Virgil as a necromancer.

Chapter Four

1. On the Sarum use, see Jacob, p. 264; Christopher Wordsworth and Henry Littlehales, *The Old Service-Books of the English Church*, 2nd ed. (London, 1910), pp. 6–9.

2. An idea of the beauty of Medieval Books of Hours can be gained from reproductions such as *The Belles Heures of Jean, Duke of Berry, Prince of France*, ed. James J. Rorimer (New York, 1958). See Duff, *Fifteenth Century English Books*, Item 174, on Caxton's *Horae ad usum Sarum*. Caxton also printed a liturgical *Psalter* in Latin [1483]; *Fifteen Oes*, a collection of prayers in English, fifteen of them beginning "O" [1491]; and one edition each of *Festum visitationis beatae virginis Mariae* [1490], *Festum transfigurationis Iesu Christi* [1490], and *Commemoratio lamentationis sive compassionis beatae Mariae* [1490].

3. Duff, *Fifteenth Century English Books*, Items 204, 207, 209, 210, 211, 212. See Crotch, p. civ, on the indulgence discovered in 1928; Wordsworth and Littlehales, pp. 286–90, on the practice of issuing indulgences; Henry

Bradshaw, *Collected Papers* (Cambridge, 1889), Paper VI, pp. 84–100, on the *Image of Pity* prints; Painter, p. 84, on what the fine print in an indulgence indicates about its promise.

4. Herbert B. Workman, *John Wyclif: A Study of the English Medieval Church*, 2 vols. in 1 (1926; rpt. Hamden, Conn., 1966) II, 15, briefly explains and documents Wyclif's objections to the issuance of indulgences.

5. The two microfilm copies of *The Book of Divers Ghostly Matters* that I examined are both from defective volumes but are ample evidence that the text is exactly what its title suggests. The phrase quoted occurs on signature A iii, v, of *Proffites of Tribulation* as reproduced by University Microfilms, Shipment 1, Reel 4, British Museum Reference Number I. A. 55141.

6. H[enry] S[tanley] Bennett, *Chaucer and the Fifteenth Century*, The Oxford History of English Literature, II, 1 (Oxford, 1947), 119, considers books of this kind the greatest manifestation of originality in the century.

7. D. W. Robertson, Jr., "The Doctrine of Charity in Mediaeval Literary Gardens: A Topical Approach through Symbolism and Allegory," *Speculum*, XXVI (1951), 24–49, sets the doctrine of *caritas* in a literary context. See p. 24 for a basic definition, drawn from St. Augustine, *De doctrina Christiana*. See also Aurelius Augustinas, *On Christian Doctrine*, ed. and trans. D. W. Robertson Jr. (New York, 1958).

8. University Microfilms, Reel 14, reproduces the British Museum copy, Reference Number C. 11. c. 5 (1) of Caxton's 1483 edition of *The Festial*. See signatures b ii, v; b 8, v; c 7, r; i 5, v–i 6, r; and n i–n ii, for the stories referred to here.

9. Blades, *Biography and Typography*, p. 326; Painter, p. 170n; however, the *Short-Title Catalogue* lists the book under Guy de Roye.

10. Workman, II, 151–55, summarizes the regular emphases of Medieval religious instruction.

11. Wilson, pp. 796–97, summarizes modern scholarship on Caxton's text of *Ars moriendi*.

12. See Baugh, pp. 288–89.

13. F. M. Ellis, ed., "Introduction," *The Golden Legend*, I (London, 1900–1922), ix-x, proposes that Caxton did not translate the entire text unaided. See also Blake, *Caxton and his World*, pp. 117–23; Painter, pp. 118, 143–46.

14. Aurner, pp. 116–17. *The Cambridge Bibliography of English Literature*, ed. F. W. Bateson, I (New York and Cambridge, 1941), 674, gives Caxton's *Golden Legend* as its first entry under *The English Bible*. *The New Cambridge Bibliography of English Literature*, I, col. 1841, however, merely notes Caxton's *Golden Legend* under "Minor Versions" of the English Bible. See also Margaret Deanesly, *The Lollard Bible and Other Medieval Biblical Versions* (Cambridge, 1920), pp. 300–302; Workman, II, 169–95; Zoltán Haraszti, "The *Catholicon*, the *Golden Legend*, and Other Early Books," *More Books*, XVI (1941), 258; David C. Fowler, "John Trevisa and the English Bible," *Modern Philology*, LVIII (1960), 81–98; David C. Fowler,

The Bible in Early English Literature (Seattle and London, 1976), pp. 17, 21, 22, 99, 157.

Chapter Five

1. See Arthur O. Lovejoy, *The Great Chain of Being* (Cambridge, Mass., 1936); Ruth Mohl, *The Three Estates in Medieval and Renaissance Literature* (New York, 1933); E. M. W. Tillyard, *The Elizabethan World Picture* (New York, 1944); E. M. W. Tillyard, *The English Renaissance: Fact or Fiction?* (Baltimore, 1952).

2. The chess pieces now called bishops are called *alphyns* (elephants) in Jacobus de Cessolis, *The Game and Play of the Chess*, tr. William Caxton, 1st ed. ([Bruges, 1475]); but, says *The Game,* they "ought to be made in the manner of Judges sitting in chair with a book open tofore [before] their eyen [eyes]" (Book II, ch. III, [folio 12, v]). See Hans Kurath and Sherman M. Kuhn, eds., *Middle English Dictionary* (Ann Arbor, 1954—), p. 518, under the spelling *aufin,* on this chess piece.

See Book II, ch. V, for the Tyberius story.

University Microfilms, Shipment 1, Reel 1, reproduces Caxton's text from the British Museum copy, Reference Number C.10.e.1. Wilson, p. 778, discusses Caxton's sources.

3. Crotch, ed., pp. 14–15.

4. Often reprinted; an accessible modern edition is Baldassare Castiglione, *The Book of the Courtier,* trans. Sir Thomas Hoby (London, 1928, rpt. 1966), the Everyman edition.

5. Arthur B. Ferguson, *The Indian Summer of English Chivalry: Studies in the Decline and Transformation of Chivalric Idealism* (Durham, N.C., 1960); Aurner, p. 187. Alfred T. P. Byles, ed., Introduction, *The Book of the Ordre of Chyualry,* Early English Text Society, Original Series, CLXVIII (London, 1926), especially pp. vii, xxxviii, discusses Caxton and the chivalric tradition.

6. Alfred T. P. Byles, ed., Introduction, *The Book of Fayttes of Armes and Chyualry by Christine de Pisan,* Early English Text Society, Original Series, CLXXXIX (London, 1932), xi–li.

7. Frederick J. Furnivall, ed., Forewords, *The Curial made by maystere Alain Charretier,* Early English Text Society, Extra Series, LIV (London, 1888; rpt. 1935, 1965). pp. vi–vii, comments on Chartier's theme of the idyllic country life set against court life in Shakespeare and some of his contemporaries. The quotation from *The Curial* occurs on p. 14 of the Furnivall edition.

8. John Lydgate, *Stans puer ad mensam,* [Westminster, 1477 or 1478], 11. 1–5. Caxton's edition is reproduced by University Microfilms, Reel 1, from a copy in Cambridge University Library. See [signature A 1, r] for the lines quoted.

9. A convenient modern edition is William Caxton, tr., *The Book of the*

Knight of the Tower, ed. M. Y. Offord, Early English Text Society, Supplementary Series II (London, New York, Toronto, 1971).

10. See ch. 74, pp. 105–106, in the Offord edition.

11. On courtly love, see C. S. Lewis, *The Allegory of Love: A Study in Medieval Tradition* (New York, 1959; originally printed, 1936), especially pp. 1–43; E. Talbot Donaldson, "The Myth of Courtly Love," *Ventures*, V, 2 (1965), 16–23, reprinted in Donaldson's *Speaking of Chaucer* (New York, 1970), pp. 154–63; F. X. Newman, ed., *The Meaning of Courtly Love, Papers of the First Annual Conference of the Center for Medieval and Early Renaissance Studies, State University of New York at Binghamton, March 17–18, 1967* (Albany, 1968), especially pp. vi–viii, 97–102.

12. L. C. Harmer, Textual Introduction, *Vocabulary in French and English*, ed. J. C. T. Oates and L. C. Harmer (Cambridge, 1964); Blake, *Caxton and his World*, p. 50. Painter, p. 103, flatly denies that the translation is Caxton's. Wilson, p. 781, reviews the question of who made the translation.

13. See Blake, *Caxton and his World*, pp. 196–97, and p. 229, Item 37, concerning the *Epitoma*, which I have not seen.

14. Walter Clyde Curry, *Chaucer and the Medieval Sciences* (New York, 1926; 2nd ed., 1960), contains much data on Medieval medicine.

Chapter Six

1. For the Scots text on which my modern English rendering is based, see David F. C. Coldwell, ed., *Selections from Gavin Douglas* (Oxford, 1964), p. 1.

2. Coldwell, p. 4.

3. Coldwell, p. 5.

4. W. [read M.] T. Culley and F[rederick] J. Furnivall, eds., *Caxton's Eneydos*, Early English Text Society, Extra Series, LVII (London, 1890), pp. 10–11.

5. I have quoted Virgil from R. D. Williams, ed., *The Aeneid of Virgil, Books 1–6* (Bassingstoke and London, 1972), p. 1.

6. Coldwell, p. 14.

7. Coldwell, p. 5.

8. Blake, ed., *Caxton's Own Prose*, pp. 55–57, gives both tales; Crotch, pp. 88–89, gives the second.

9. S. Gaselee and H. F. B. Brett-Smith, eds., Introduction, *Ovyde: Hys Booke of Metamorphose, Books X–XV* (Oxford, 1924), p. xxi.

10. Gaselee and Brett-Smith, Book XII, ch. 10, p. 77.

11. See the *Short-Title Catalogue* for editions of *Blanchardin and Eglantine*.

12. Aurner, p. 185; Charles Knight, *William Caxton, The First English Printer* (London, 1877), p. 134; George Putnam, *Books and Their Makers During the Middle Ages* (New York and London, 1897), II, 127.

13. Wilson, p. 782.

14. Mary Noyes Colvin, ed., *Godeffroy of Boloyne, or the Siege and Conquest of Jerusalem*, Early English Text Society, Extra Series, LXIV (London, 1893), p. viii.

15. Sir Thomas Malory, *The Winchester Malory, A Facsimile*, ed. N. R. Ker, Early English Text Society, Supplementary Series, IV (London, New York, Toronto, 1976); Sir Thomas Malory, *Le Morte d'Arthur, Printed by William Caxton, 1485*, ed. Paul Needham (London, 1976).

16. Crotch omits part of the Prologue and all the Epilogue to *Le Morte d'Arthur*. These can be found in various editions, including Blake, *Caxton's Own Prose*, pp. 106–11; see pp. 110–11 for the Epilogue.

17. Eugène Vinaver, ed., *The Works of Sir Thomas Malory*, 2nd ed., 3 vols. (Oxford, 1967, rpt. 1973); R. M. Lumiansky, ed., *Malory's Originality: A Critical Study of "Le Morte Darthur"* (Baltimore, 1964); Blake, *Caxton and his World*, pp. 108–13; Walter F. Oakeshott, "Caxton and Malory's *Morte Darthur*," *Gutenberg-Jahrbuch* (1935), pp. 112–16.

18. The Early English Text Society edition of *The Winchester Malory*, folio 148, v, shows this passage in facsimile. The Vinaver edition, I, 371, provides a convenient typeface with some punctuation and expansion of contractions. The Needham edition of the Caxton *Morte d'Arthur*, leaf 136, v, and leaf 137, r, provides a facsimile which may be compared with the edition by H. Oskar Sommer, *Le Morte Darthur by Syr Thomas Malory* (London, 1889; rpt. New York, 1973), I, 272–73.

19. Vinaver, I, [181]–247.

20. John Milton, *Areopagitica* (London, 1644), often reprinted; see, for example, Frank Allen Patterson, gen. ed., *The Works of John Milton*, IV (New York, 1931), 310.

21. G. C. Maccaulay, ed., Introduction, *The Complete Works of John Gower*, II (Oxford, 1901), clxviii–clxix; and John H. Fisher, *John Gower, Moral Philosopher and Friend of Chaucer* (New York, 1964), pp. 8–12, discuss Caxton's text.

22. The translation and any faults in it are my own. I am grateful, however, to Dr. Joseph S. White of the Department of Classical Studies, University of Richmond, for assistance with it.

23. These lines appear in many editions of Chaucer's *Book* (or *House*) *of Fame* and in Blake, *Caxton's Own Prose*, p. 102.

24. On Caxton's two editions of *The Canterbury Tales*, see Aurner, pp. 165–68; Thomas F. Dunn, *The Manuscript Source of Caxton's Second Edition of "The Canterbury Tales"* (Chicago, 1940); Blake, *Caxton and his World*, pp. 101–108; Painter, p. 91. See further Walter L. Heilbronner, *Printing and the Book in Fifteenth-Century England: A Bibliographical Survey* (Charlottesville, Va., 1967). The lines quoted here and below are, respectively, from Caxton's first and second editions of *The Canterbury Tales* as reproduced by University Microfilms, Shipment 1, Reel 4, from British Museum Reference Number 167. c. 26, folios 1, r, and 4, v, and Shipment 1,

Reel 1, from British Museum Reference Number C. 11586, signatures a iii, r, and a 7, v–a 8, r. Further comparison of texts may be made in John M. Manly and Edith Rickert, eds., *The Text of the Canterbury Tales*, 8 vols. (Chicago, 1940). Modern editions usually supply both a standard text to which Caxton's may be compared and commentary on Chaucer's pronunciation, of which my analysis represents a conservative view.

25. See Germaine Dempster, "The Fifteenth-Century Editors of the *Canterbury Tales* and the Problem of Tale Order," *Publications of The Modern Language Association of America*, LXIV (1949), 1123–42.

Chapter Seven

1. See Wilson, pp. 776–802, on Caxton's translations and their sources; Crotch, and Blake, *Caxton's Own Prose*, for texts of Caxton's original writing and comment thereon; Wilson, pp. 802–807, for a bibliography of Caxton's original writing. Modern editions of Caxton's translations generally offer some introductory comment on his style; Wilson, 927–30, supplies bibliography of analyses of Caxton's style. See the Primary Bibliography for Caxton's translations and for his editions which contain prologues and epilogues.

2. Crotch, pp. 2–3, shows Caxton's and Lefèvre's texts.

3. See Blake, *Caxton's Own Prose*, pp. 32–43, on "Caxton's Language." See also Leon Kellner, ed., "Introduction on Caxton's Syntax, Style, Etc.," *Caxton's Blanchardyn and Eglantine*, Early English Text Society, Extra Series, LVIII (London, 1890; rpt. 1962), xxxii–xxxv.

4. I am using the system set forth in Homer C. House and Susan Emolyn Harman, *Descriptive English Grammar*, 2nd ed. (Englewood Cliffs, N.J., 1950).

5. The Dutch is from J. W. Muller and H. Logeman, eds., *Die Hystorie van Reynaert die Vos, naar den druk van 1479, vergeleken met William Caxton's Engelsche vertaling* (Zwolle, 1892), p. [7]; the English from University Microfilms, Reel 12, from the British Museum copy, Reference Number 1. B. 55040, signature A 4, r. See also N. F. Blake, ed., *The History of Reynard the Fox, Translated from the Dutch Original by William Caxton*, Early English Text Society, Original Series, CCLXVI (London, New York, Toronto, 1970), pp. 6, 7.

Chapter Eight

1. See Blake, *Reynard*, p. 140.

2. See Crotch, pp. 50–53, for the French and English texts.

3. See Crotch, pp. 20–31, for the Socratic dicts; p. 24 for the dict quoted. Crotch, pp. cviii–cix, cxiv, comments on Caxton's humor.

4. Crotch, p. cxxiv, reprints de Worde's colophon.

5. William Shakespeare, *Hamlet*, Act II, Scene II, ll. 415–19, in Craig, p. 917.

6. John Donne, "The Sun Rising," 1. 1, in Herbert J. C. Grierson, ed., *The Poems of John Donne*, I (London, 1912, rpt. 1966), p. 1; Geoffrey Chaucer, *Troilus and Criseyde*, Book III, 1. 1465, in John H. Fisher, ed. *The Complete Poetry and Prose of Geoffrey Chaucer* (New York, 1977), p. 476 (my modernization).

7. These comparisons are based on Duff, *Fifteenth Century English Books;* and Pollard and Redgrave, *A Short-Title Catalogue*. The data cannot be totally accurate. Some editions have totally disappeared, and some items overlooked by Duff and by Pollard and Redgrave have since been discovered. The lists they offer, however, are sufficiently comprehensive and representative to yield reliable evidence. Lucien Febvre and Henri-Jean Martin, *L'apparition du livre*, L'évolution de l'humanité, fondée par Henri Berr (Paris, 1958), pp. 256–325, provides a European background against which the English scene may be viewed. See Blake, *Caxton: England's First Publisher*, p. 185, for a rather different summation from mine.

8. As Duff, *Fifteenth Century English Books*, states concerning Item 101, the St. Albans *Chronicles*, incunabula of the same titles do not always have the same content.

9. In 1635, *Troilus* achieved the dignity of a Latin translation. See *A Short-Title Catalogue*, No. 5097.

Selected Bibliography

PRIMARY SOURCES

Authors and titles of books printed by Caxton occur in various forms; I have generally given both as they appear in *The New Cambridge Bibliography of English Literature*. I have generally limited the reprints and editions to those I have used, including microfilms by University Microfilms, Ann Arbor, Michigan, of items in the Pollard and Redgrave *Short-Title Catalogue*, identified by reel number and the name of the library holding the copy filmed.

There is no perfect agreement on dating if Caxton did not give a date of publication. Because George D. Painter has made a recent examination and evaluation of the evidence available for dating, I follow his order of probable publication (*William Caxton*, pp. 211–15), with the addition of one title, *De proprietatibus rerum*. Dates in the body of my book follow Painter. Here, however, for books of inferential date, I give Painter's; then after a semicolon, Duff's, from *Fifteenth Century English Books* (hereafter cited as Duff); then after a second semicolon, the date from *The New Cambridge Bibliography of English Literature*. *The New Cambridge Bibliography* supplies identifications of miscellaneous pieces in certain Caxton editions, as noted here.

I have followed Wilson, pp. 776–802, on Caxton's sources, except as noted in individual items. The most recent assessment of what work constitutes Caxton's own composition has been made by N. F. Blake in his edition of *Caxton's Own Prose;* I follow Wilson and Blake in attributing original composition to Caxton. If second and later editions of a given work merely repeat Caxton's free composition from the first edition with trifling variants, I omit repeated notice of Caxton's composition in entering these later editions.

A few Bruges books which are perhaps Mansion's rather than Caxton's, and the few very rare Caxtons which I did not examine personally are marked not seen. If no author is named, the book is anonymous.

Cologne

BARTHOLOMAEUS ANGLICUS. *De proprietatibus rerum.* [Printer of the Flores S. Augustini, 1471]. Perhaps the text on which Caxton learned to print.

Bruges

LEFÈVRE, RAOUL. *The Recuyell of the Historyes of Troye,* tr. William Caxton. [1475; 1475; 1473/4]. Ascribed to Caxton and Mansion. Translated from the French *Le recueil des histoires de Troyes,* together with a version of Guido delle Colonne, *Historia trojana.* Contains Caxton's Preface; Prologue; Conclusion to Book II; Epilogue to Book II; General Epilogue.

———. Ed. H. Oskar Sommer. 2 vols. London: David Nutt, 1894.

———. Ed. H. Halliday Sparling. 3 vols. in 2. Hammersmith: Kelmscott Press, 1892.

CESSOLIS, JACOBUS de. *The Game and Play of the Chess,* tr. William Caxton. 1st ed. [After 31 March 1475; 1476; 1475/6]. Usually ascribed to Mansion and Caxton. Translated from *Liber de moribus* as translated from the Latin of Jacobus de Cessolis into French by Jean Ferron and Jean de Vignay. Contains Caxton's Prologue; Additions to Book 3, Chapters 2 and 3 and to Book IV, Chapter 1; Epilogue. University Microfilms, Shipment 1, Reel 1, British Museum.

LEFÈVRE, RAOUL. *Le recueil des histoires de Troyes* [1475; 1477; 1475/6]. Often ascribed to Mansion, not Caxton.

d'AILLY, PIERRE. *Septenuaire de pseaulmes de penitence.* [1475; 1477, 1475/6]. Attributed to Mansion by Duff. Not seen.

LEFÈVRE, RAOUL. *Le recueil des histoires de Troyes* [1475; 1477; 1475/6]. Attributed to Mansion by Duff. Not seen.

MIELOT, JEAN, tr. *Les quatre choses derrenieres.* [1476; 1476; 1475/6]. Duff, Item 108, and Painter ascribe to Caxton. De Ricci, *A Census of Caxtons,* Item 2, suggests that it may not be his.

Westminster

Indulgence, POPE SIXTUS IV. [Westminster (?), 1476; not in Duff; not in *New Cambridge Bibliography*].

BURGH, BENET, tr. *Parvus Cato; Magnus Cato,* ascribed to "Dionysius Cato." 1st ed. [1476; n.d.; 1477].

———. Facsimile. Ed. Francis Jenkinson. Cambridge: University Press, 1906.

LYDGATE, JOHN. *The Churl and the Bird.* 1st ed. [1476; n.d.; 1477]. Neither of the two editions is dated, contributing to uncertainty as to which is the first. University Microfilms, Reel 1, British Museum.

———. Facsimile. Ed. F. Jenkinson, Cambridge: University Press, 1906.

LYDGATE, JOHN. *The Horse, Sheep, and Goose. 1st ed.* [1476; n.d.; 1477]. Also in two undated editions. University Microfilms, Reel 1, Cambridge University Library.

LEFÈVRE, RAOUL. *The History of Jason,* tr. William Caxton. [1477; 1477; 1479]. Translated from the French *Jason et Medee,* with additions from

Boccaccio, *Genealogia deorum*. Contains Caxton's Prologue; Note to
Lefèvre's Prologue; Epilogue. University Microfilms, Reel 47.

———. Ed. John Munro, Early English Text Society, Extra Series, CXI.
London: Kegan Paul, Trench, Trübner & Co. Ltd.; Humphrey Milford,
Oxford University Press, 1913.

TIGNONVILLE, GUILLAUME de. *The Dicts or Sayings of the Philosophers*, tr.
Anthony Woodville, Earl Rivers. 1st ed. 1477. The ultimate source is
al-Mubashshir ibn Fatik, *Mukhtar al-hikam;* see Farrar and Evans, Item
2816; *British Museum, Catalogue*. Contains Caxton's Epilogue; Colophon. University Microfilms, Shipment 1, Reel 4, British Museum.

———. Facsimile, with a preface by William Blades. London: Elliot Stock,
1877.

CHRISTINE de PISAN. *The Moral Proverbs*, tr. Anthony Woodville, Earl
Rivers. 1478. Contains Caxton's Epilogue; Colophon.

———. Facsimile. Ed. William Blades. London: Blades, East, & Blades,
1859.

BURGH, BENET, tr. *Parvus Cato; Magnus Cato*. 2nd ed. [1477 or 1478; n.d.;
1477].

CHAUCER, GEOFFREY. *The Temple of Brass (Parliament of Fowls); A
Treatise Which John Scogan Sent; The Good Counsel of Chaucer;
Balade of a Village; Th'Envoy of Chaucer*. [1477 or 1478; n.d.; 1477].
University Microfilms, Reel 1, Cambridge University Library.

CHAUCER, GEOFFREY. *Anelida and the False Arcyte; The Complaint of
Chaucer to his Purse; Th'Envoy of Chaucer*. [1477 or 1478; n.d.; 1477].
University Microfilms, Reel 1, Cambridge University Library.

———. Facsimile. Ed. F. Jenkinson. Cambridge, Eng.: University Press,
1905.

The Book of Courtesy. [1477 or 1478; 1477 or 1478; 1477/8].

———. Ed. Frederick J. Furnivall, Early English Text Society, Extra Series,
III. London: Kegan Paul, Trench, Trübner, & Co., 1868; rpt. 1882,
1898.

LYDGATE, JOHN. *The Churl and the Bird*. 2nd ed. [1477 or 1478; n.d.; 1477].

LYDGATE, JOHN. *The Horse, Sheep, and Goose*. 2nd ed. [1477 or 1478; n.d.;
1477].

LYDGATE, JOHN. *Stans puer ad mensam*, with the anonymous *An Holy Salve
Regina*. [1477 or 1478; n.d.; 1477]. University Microfilms, Reel 1,
Cambridge University Library.

LYDGATE, JOHN. *The Temple of Glass*. [1477 or 1478; n.d.; 1477 or 1478].
University Microfilms, Reel 1, Cambridge University Library.

———. Facsimile. Cambridge: University Press, 1905.

Horae ad usum Sarum. 1st ed. [1477 or 1478; 1477 or 1478; 1477].

Infantia salvatoris. [1477 or 1478; n.d.; 1477]. In Latin.

RUSSELL, JOHN. *Propositio clarissimi oratoris magistri Johannis Russell*.
[1477 or 1478; n.d.; Bruges or Westminster, 1476]. In Latin.

CHAUCER, GEOFFREY. *The Canterbury Tales*. 1st ed. [1478; 1478; 1478].

The first edition of *The Canterbury Tales* ever printed. University Microfilms, Shipment 1, Reel 4, British Museum.

CHAUCER, GEOFFREY, tr. *Boethius de consolatione philosophiae*. [1478; before 1479; 1478]. Contains Caxton's Epilogue. University Microfilms, Reel 1, British Museum.

VAN VLIEDERHOVEN, GERARD. *The Cordial*, tr. Anthony Woodville, Earl Rivers. 1479. Contains Caxton's Epilogue. University Microfilms, Reel 2, British Museum.

TRAVERSAGNI, LAURENTIUS GULIELMUS de SAONA. *Nova rhetorica*. [1479; 1479; 1479]. Not seen.

Ordinale secundum usum Sarum. [1479; 1477; 1477]. William Blades (see *Biography and Typography*, pp. 215–16) discovered a copy of Caxton's *Boethius*, still in the original binding. The binding yielded fragments of thirteen other Caxtons, three of them—a *Horae*, an *Indulgence*, and this *Ordinale*—previously unknown. For the text of the *Ordinale* and comment on it, see *The Tracts of Clement Maydeston with the Remains of Caxton's Ordinale*, ed. C. Wordsworth, Henry Bradshaw Society . . . for the editing of Rare Liturgical Texts, VII (London, 1894), 91–116.

CAXTON, WILLIAM. *Advertisement*. [1479; 1477; 1477]. Duff, Item 80, and others give the complete text. See also *Caxton's Advertisement: Photolithograph of the copy preserved in the Bodleian Library, Oxford . . .* , ed. Edward W.B. Nicholson, London: Bernard Quaritch; Oxford: Clarendon Press [1892].

Horae ad usum Sarum. 2nd ed. [1479;1480;1480].

TIGNONVILLE, GUILLAUME de. *The Dicts or Sayings of the Philosophers*, tr. Anthony Woodville, Earl Rivers. 2nd ed. [1480; n.d.]; 1479. University Microfilms, Shipment 1, Reel 4, British Museum.

TRAVERSAGNI, LAURENTIUS GULIELMUS de SAONA. *Epitoma sive isagogicum margarite castigate eloquentie*. [1480; not in Duff; 1480]. Not seen. Consult José Ruysschaert, "Les manuscrits autographes de deux oeuvres de Lorenzo Gugielmo Traversagni imprimées chez Caxton," *Bulletin of the John Rylands Library*, XXXVI (1953–54), 191–97.

Indulgence, Pope Sixtus IV. [Not after 31 March 1480; 1480; not in *New Cambridge Bibliography*]. See Duff for the text of this and later indulgences.

Festum visitationis beatae virginis Mariae (Officium Visitationis B.V.M.). [1480; n.d.; 1480]. Not seen.

CAXTON, WILLIAM, tr. (?). *Vocabulary in French and English*. [1480; 1480; 1480]. Also called by editors *Book for Travellers*, or *Doctrine to Learn French and English*. Translated from *Livre des mestiers de Bruges*, a French-Flemish phrase book here made into a French-English one. Attribution of the translation to Caxton is uncertain. Contains Caxton's colophon. University Microfilms, Reel 159, Huntington Library.

———. Ed. Henry Bradley. Early English Text Society, Extra Series, LXXIX. London: Kegan Paul, Trench, Trübner & Co., Ltd., 1900.

154WILLIAM CAXTON

————. Facsimile. Ed. J. C. T. Oates and L. C. Harmer. Cambridge: University Press, 1964.

Chronicles of England. 1st ed. 1480. Contain Caxton's Prologue; Table of Contents; Conclusion; Colophon.

HIGDEN, RANULF. *The Decription of Britain,* tr. John Trevisa. Extracted from *Polychronicon,* William Caxton. 1480. Contains Caxton's Prologue; Epilogue. University Microfilms, Reel 13, British Museum.

Indulgence, Pope Sixtus IV. [Not before 7 August 1480]; 1480; not in *New Cambridge Bibliography.*

GOSSOUIN (GAUTIER?) de METZ. *The Mirror of the World,* tr. William Caxton. 1st ed. [After 8 March 1481; 1481; 1481]. Formerly attributed to Vincent of Beauvais. Translated from a prose *Image du monde,* which is in turn from a verse *Image du monde,* the poem or the poem and the prose version by Gossouin or Gautier de Metz. Contains Caxton's Introduction; Prologue; Additions to Book II, Chapters xi, xii, xiv, xv, and to Book III, Chapter xxiv; Epilogue.

————. Ed. Oliver H. Prior. Early English Text Society, Extra Series, CX. London: Kegan Paul, Trench, Trübner & Co., Ltd.; London and New York: Humphrey Milford, Oxford University Press, 1913 (for 1912); reissued by Oxford University Press, 1966.

CAXTON, WILLIAM, tr. *Reynard the Fox.* 1st ed. [After 6 June 1481; After 6 June 1481; 1481]. Translated from the Dutch *Hystorie van Reynaert die Vos* which itself has a complex history of sources. Contains Caxton's Epilogue. University Microfilms, Reel 12, British Museum.

————. Ed. Donald B. Sands. Cambridge, Mass.: Harvard University Press; London: Oxford University Press, 1960.

————. Ed. N.F. Blake. Early English Text Society, Original Series, CCLXIII. London, etc.: Oxford University Press, 1970.

CICERO, MARCUS TULLIUS. *Of Old Age,* tr. John Tiptoft, Earl of Worcester (?) with corrections by William Caxton. Cicero. *Of Friendship,* tr. John Tiptoft. Bonaccursius de Montemagno. *The Declamation of Noblesse,* tr. John Tiptoft. 1481. Contains Caxton's Proem; Colophon to *Of Old Age;* Prologue; Epilogue to *Of Friendship;* one sentence Preface; Epilogue to *Of Noblesse.* University Microfilms, Reel 11, British Museum.

————. "Caxton: Tulle of Olde Age," ed. Heinz Susebach. In *Textuntersuchung mit Literarischer Einführung, Studien zur Englischen Philologie,* LXXV. Halle: Max Niemeyer, 1933.

Indulgence, Pope Sixtus IV. [Not before 7 August 1481; 1481; not in *New Cambridge Bibliography.* Two: Duff items 209 and 210.

CAXTON, WILLIAM, tr. *Godfrey of Boloyne.* 1481. Also called *Seige and Conquest of Jerusalem* or *Eracles.* Translated from *Estoire de Eracles* [Heraclius] *empereur et la conqueste de la terre d'outremer,* itself translated from William of Tyre, *Historia rerum in partibus transmarinis gestarum,* with various accretions. Contains Caxton's Prologue; Epilogue. University Microfilms, Reel 12, British Museum.

————. Ed. Mary Noyes Colvin. Early English Text Society, Extra Series, LXIV. London: Kegan Paul, Trench, Trübner & Co., 1893.

Chronicles of England. 2nd ed. 1482. University Microfilms, Reel 3, British Museum.

HIGDEN, RANULF. *Polychronicon,* tr. John Trevisa and "a little embellished" by William Caxton. [1482; 1482; 1482]. Contains Caxton's Proem, Epilogue to Book 7; Prologue and Epilogue to Book 8. University Microfilms, Reel 13, British Museum.

BURGH, BENET, tr. *Parvus Cato; Magnus Cato.* 3rd ed. [1482; n d.]; 1481. University Microfilms, Reel 1, British Museum.

CESSOLIS, JACOBUS de. *The Game and Play of the Chess.* 2nd ed. [1482; n.d.; 1483]. Printed, Caxton says, because the first edition sold out. Caxton's Prologue is significantly modified by the omission of the dedication to George, Duke of Clarence, which appears in the first edition; new conclusion. University Microfilms, Shipment 1, Reel 1, British Museum.

Psalter. [1483; n.d.; 1480]. University Microfilms, Xerox book of British Museum copy.

De curia sapienciae. [1483; 1480; 1480]. Sometimes, apparently erroneously, ascribed to John Lydgate—an error Caxton did not commit. University Microfilms, Reel 1, British Museum.

DEGUILLEVILLE, GUILLAUME. *The Pilgrimage of the Soul,* tr. anonymous. 1483. Translation formerly ascribed to John Lydgate. Contains Caxton's Incipit; Explicit. University Microfilms, Reel 15, St. John's College, Oxford.

MIRK, JOHN. *The Festial (Liber Festivalis).* 1st ed. 1483; 1483; [1483]. University Microfilms, Reel 14, British Museum.

MIRK, JOHN. *Four Sermons (Quattuor Sermones).* 1st ed. [1483; 1483; not entered separately to *The Festial* in *New Cambridge Bibliography*]. See Painter, pp. 213, 215; and Blake, *Caxton: England's First Publisher,* pp. 92–95, on the recognition of the "first" edition of *Four Sermons* as actually two.

GOWER, JOHN. *Confessio amantis.* 1483; 14[8]3; 1483. The date Caxton gives, 1493, is in error, apparently by ten years. Contains Caxton's Prologue; Table of Contents; Colophon. University Microfilms, Reel 50, British Museum.

CHARTIER, ALAIN. *The Curial,* tr. William Caxton. [1483; 1484; 1484]. Translated from *De vita curiali,* in a French text. Contains Caxton's Prologue; Colophon. University Microfilms, Reel 16, British Museum.

————. Ed. Frederick J. Furnivall and Paul Meyer Early English Text Society, Extra Series, LIV. London: Humphrey Milford, Oxford University Press, 1888; rpt. 1935, 1965.

CHAUCER, GEOFFREY. *The Canterbury Tales.* 2nd ed. [1483; n.d.; 1484]. Contains Caxton's Proem. University Microfilms, Shipment 1, Reel 1, British Museum.

CHAUCER, GEOFFREY. *The Book of Fame.* [1483; n.d.; 1483]. Contains Caxton's Incipit; Conclusion (in verse); Epilogue. University Microfilms, Reel 1, Cambridge University Library.

CHAUCER, GEOFFREY. *Troilus and Criseyde.* [1483; n.d.; 1483]. University Microfilms, Shipment 1, Reel 1, British Museum.

LYDGATE, JOHN. *The Life of Our Lady.* [1483; 1484; 1484]. Contains Caxton's Epilogue (in English verse and Latin prose). University Microfilms, Reel 1, British Museum.

CARMELIANO, PIETRO. *Sex epistolae.* [1483; 1483; 1483]. Contains Caxton's Colophon (in Latin).

———. Facsimile reproduced by James Hyatt. Tr. George Bullen. London: Lawrence & Bullen, 1892.

LA TOUR LANDRY, GEOFFROY de. *The Knight of the Tower,* tr. William Caxton. 1484. Translated from *Livre . . . pour l'enseignement de ses filles.* Contains Caxton's Prologue; Colophon. University Microfilms, Reel 16, British Museum.

———. Ed. M.Y. Offord. Early English Text Society, Supplementary Series, II. London, etc.: Oxford University Press, 1971.

CAXTON, WILLIAM, tr. *Caton (Parvus Cato; Magnus Cato,* ascribed to "Dionysius Cato"). 4th ed. [1484; 1483; 1483]. Only edition of Caxton's own translation, made from a French *Cathon* with materials not appearing in the Latin *Disticha Catonis* from which Benet Burgh translated and which Caxton also printed. Contains Caxton's Prologue; Table of Contents with Note; Colophon. University Microfilms, Reel 9, Cambridge University Library.

MIRK, JOHN. *Four Sermons,* 2nd ed. [1484; not recognized in Duff; not recognized in *New Cambridge Bibliography*].

CAXTON, WILLIAM, tr. *Fables of Aesop.* 1484. Translated from Julien Macho, *Subtilles fables de Esope,* derived from Heinrich Steinhöwel, and ultimately from a complex of sources. Contains Caxton's Incipit; Epilogue; two brief stories, the first at the conclusion of the other fables and the second embedded in the Epilogue. University Microfilms, Reel 16, British Museum.

———. Ed. R. T. Lenaghan. Cambridge, Mass.: Harvard University Press, 1967.

LULL, RAMON. *The Book of the Order of Chivalry or Knighthood,* tr. William Caxton. [1484; 1484; 1484]. Translated from *Livre de l'ordre de chevalerie,* itself translated from Ramon Lull, *Libre del orde de cauayleria.* Contains Caxton's Epilogue. University Microfilms, Shipment 1, Reel 4, British Museum.

———. Ed. Alfred T. P. Byles. Early English Text Society, Original Series, CLXVIII. London: Humphrey Milford, Oxford University Press, 1926.

VARAGINE, JACOBUS de. *The Golden Legend,* tr. William Caxton. [1484;

After 20 November 1483; 1483]. Translated from the Latin of Jacobus de
Varagine, *Legenda aurea*, together with a French version of *Legenda
aurea* by Jean de Vignay and an English translation, *Gilte Legende*.
Contains Caxton's Prologue; eleven additions to lives; Epilogue.

————. Ed. F. S. Ellis. 7 vols. London: J. M. Dent & Sons Ltd., Aldine
House, 1900-1922.

MALORY, SIR THOMAS. *Le Morte d'Arthur*. 1485. Contains Caxton's Pro
logue; Table of Contents; Epilogue. Numerous editions, not necessarily
very faithful. A careful reproduction of Caxton's text was edited by H.
Oskar Sommer, 3 vols., London: David Nutt, 1889-91, rpt. New York.
AMS Press, 1973. A facsimile of the Pierpont Morgan Library incunabulum, with an introduction by Paul Needham, has been issued by
The Scolar Press (London, 1976).

CAXTON, WILLIAM, tr. *The Life of Charles the Great*. 1485. Translated from
Fier a bras by Jean Bagnyon (?) and Vincent of Beauvais's *Speculum*.
Contains Caxton's Prologue; Envoy. University Microfilms, Reel 16,
British Museum.

————. Ed. Sidney J. H. Herrtage. Early English Text Society, Extra Series,
XXXVI, XXXVII. London: N. Trübner & Co., 1880, 1881.

CAXTON, WILLIAM, tr. *Paris and Vienne*. 1485. Translated from a French
Paris et Vienne, with Provencal and Catalan (?) antecedents. Contains
Caxton's Colophon. University Microfilms, Reel 16, British Museum.

————. Ed. MacEdward Leach. Early English Text Society, Original Series,
CCXXXIV. London, etc.: Oxford University Press, 1957 (for 1951).

MAYDESTON, CLEMENT. *Directorium sacerdotum*. 1st ed. [1486; 1487;
1487]. See *The Tracts of Clement Maydeston* . . . , ed. C. Wordsworth,
vols. XX, XXII (1901, 1902).

Image of Pity. 1st ed. [1486; not in Duff; 1487]. Inserted in the British
Museum copy of Maydeston, *Directorium*. See Blades, *Biography and
Typography*, p. 324.

Horae ad usum Sarum. 3rd ed. [1486; 1490; 1489].

LOVE, NICOLAS, tr. *The Mirror of the Life of Christ (Speculum vitae Christi)*.
1st ed. [1486; 1486; 1486]. See Samuel K. Workman, *Fifteenth Century
Translation as an Influence on English Prose*, Princeton Studies in
English, XVIII (Princeton, N.J., 1940), p. 173. University Microfilms,
Reel 17, Cambridge University Library.

LORENS d'ORLEANS. *The Royal Book*, tr. William Caxton. [1487; 1486;
1484?] Translated from *Somme (Livre) des vices et des vertus*, or *Somme
le roi*. Contains Caxton's Prologue; Epilogue. University Microfilms,
Reel 17, British Museum.

VARAGINE, JACOBUS de. *The Golden Legend*, tr. William Caxton. 2nd ed.
[1487; 1487?; 1487]. Painter, p. 156, denies that this is a true second
edition.

Deathbed Prayers. [1487? or 1485?; n.d.; 1482]. Blades, *Biography and
Typography*, pp. 285–86, gives the text.

PRIOR ROBERT of SHREWSBURY (?). *The Life of Saint Winifred*, tr. William

Caxton. [1487? or 1485?; 1485; 1485]. The Latin text from which Caxton translated is doubtfully ascribed to Prior Robert. Contains Caxton's Conclusion. University Microfilms, Reel 16, British Museum.

———. Ed. C. Horstmann. *Anglia*, III (1880), 293–316.

DONATUS, AELIUS. *Donatus melior*, revised Antonio Mancinello. [1487; 1487; 1487]. Not seen.

LEGRAND, JACQUES. *The Book of Good Manners*, tr. William Caxton. 1487. Translated from *Livre de bonnes moeurs*. Contains Caxton's Prologue; Colophon. University Microfilms, Reel 17, British Museum.

Missale ad usum Sarum. Paris, 1487. Not in *New Cambridge Bibliography*. Printed by Guillaume Maynyal for Caxton; first use of Caxton's device. Not seen.

Legenda secundum usum Sarum. [Paris]: 1488; [1487; not in *New Cambridge Bibliography*]. Printed by Guillaume Maynyal in Paris for Caxton. Not seen.

CAXTON, WILLIAM, tr. *Reynard the Fox*. 2nd ed. [1488; 1489; 1489]. Handwritten Epilogue in the second edition is doubtfully attributed to Caxton. University Microfilms, Reel 14, Pepysian Library, Cambridge.

MAYDESTON, CLEMENT. *Directorium sacerdotum*. 2nd ed. [1488; 1489; 1489]. University Microfilms, Reel 124, Bodleian Library, Oxford.

CAXTON, WILLIAM, tr. *Four Sons of Aymon*. [1488; 1489; 1489]. Translated from the *chanson de geste* called *Les quatre fils Aymon* in a prose version. Contains Caxton's Prologue; Colophon.

———. Ed. Octavia Richardson. Early English Text Society, Extra Series, XLIV, XLV. London: N. Trübner & Co., 1884, 1885.

CAXTON, WILLIAM, tr. *Blanchardin and Eglantine*. [1488; 1489; 1489]. Translated from the French *Blancandin*. Contains Caxton's Prologue.

———. Ed. Leon Kellner. Early English Text Society, Extra Series, LVIII. London: N. Trübner & Co., 1890; rpt. 1962.

TIGNONVILLE, GUILLAUME de. *The Dicts or Sayings of the Philosophers*, tr. Anthony Woodville, Earl Rivers. 3rd ed. [1489; 1489; 1489].

Indulgence, Pope Innocent VIII. [Not after 24 April 1489; Before 24 April 1489; not in *New Cambridge Bibliography*].

Indulgence, Pope Innocent VIII. [1489; 1489; not in *New Cambridge Bibliography*].

CHRISTINE de PISAN. *The Book of the Feats of Arms and Chivalry*, tr. William Caxton. 1489; 1489; 1489–90. Translated from Christine's translation, *Livre des faiz darmes et de chevallerie*. Contains Caxton's Epilogue. University Microfilms, Reel 1, British Museum.

———. Ed. A. T. P. Byles. Early English Text Society, Original Series. CLXXXIX. London: H. Milford, Oxford University Press, 1932.

CAXTON, WILLIAM, tr. *Doctrinal of Sapience*. [After 7 May 1489; After 7 May 1489; 1489]. Translated from *Doctrinal aux simples gens (de sapience)*, said in the Prologue which Caxton translated to have been written by Guy de Roye but considered by modern scholars to be anonymous. Contains Caxton's Prologue; Colophon; brief printed note added to one known copy, introducing an additional chapter: "This chapter tofore I durst not set in the book because it is not convenient nor appertaining [suitable] that every layman should know it. . . ." The chapter has to do with accidents which may occur during mass and how to cope with them. See Blake, *Caxton's Own Prose*, p. 78; Painter, pp. 170, 172. University Microfilms, Reel 143, Huntington Library.

GOSSOUIN (GAUTIER?) de METZ. *The Mirror of the World*, tr. William Caxton. 2nd ed. [1489; 1490; 1490]. University Microfilms, Reel 17.

Statutes of Henry VII. [1490; 1489; 1489]. University Microfilms, Xerox book.

CAXTON, WILLIAM, tr. *Eneydos.* [After 22 June 1490; After 22 June 1490; 1490]. Translated from a French prose version, *Livre des Eneydes,* derived in part, possibly directly, from Virgil, but more significantly from Boccaccio, *De casibus,* and other Troy materials (see Wilson, p. 799). Contains Caxton's Prologue; Colophon. University Microfilms, Reel 17, British Museum.

———. Ed. W. [read M.] T. Culley and F. J. Furnivall. Early English Text Society, Extra Series, LVII. London: N. Trübner & Co., 1890.

LOVE, NICOLAS, tr. *The Mirror of the Life of Christ (Speculum vitae Christi).* 2nd ed. [1490; 1490; 1490]. University Microfilms, Reel 16, British Museum.

Horae ad usum Sarum. 4th ed. [1490; 1490; 1490].

Festum transfigurationis Jesu Christi (Officium Transfigurationis Jesu Christi). [1490; n.d.; 1491]. Not seen.

Commemoratio lamentationis sive compassionis beatae Mariae. [1490; 1490; 1487].

———. Facsimile. Ed. E. Gordon Duff. Oxford: University Press, 1901.

Image of Pity. 2nd ed. [1490?; not in Duff; 1490]. De Ricci, *Census,* Item 55, calls this a xylographic imitation of Caxton's type 5 and dates it *c.* 1490.

CAXTON, WILLIAM, tr. *The Art and Craft to Know Well to Die.* [After 15 June 1490; After 15 June 1490; 1490]. Translated from *Traite de bien mourir,* in turn from *Tractatus artis bene moriendi.* Contains Caxton's Incipit; Explicit. For the texts of *The Art and Craft* and of *Ars moriendi,* below, see F. M. M. Comper, ed., *The Book of the Craft of Dying . . . ,* London: Longmans, Green, & Co. 1917.

Governal of Health; Medicina stomachi. [1491; 1489; 1489]. University Microfilms, Reel 67, Bodleian Library, Oxford.

The Book of Divers Ghostly Matters. [1491; 1491; 1491]. In three parts. Contains Caxton's Incipit and Colophon to Part One, *Horologium;* Prologue and Conclusion to Part Three, *The Rule of St. Benedict.* (See Blake, *Caxton's Own Prose*, pp. 101–102). For Part One, Henricus Suso, *Horologium sapientiae,* see Carl Horstmann, ed., *Anglia,* X (1888), 323–89; for Part Two, *The Twelve Profits of Tribulation,* see Carl Horstmann, ed., *Yorkshire Writers,* Library of Early English Writers, II

(London: Swan Sonnenschein, 1895–96), 45–60 (not seen); for Part
Three, *The Rule of St. Benedict,* see E. A. Kock, ed., *Three Middle-
English Versions of the Rule of St. Benet* . . . , Early English Text
Society, Original Series, CXX (London: Kegan Paul, Trench, Trübner &
Co., Ltd., 1902). University Microfilms, Reel 1, Cambridge University
Library (?); Shipment 1, Reel 1, British Museum.

CAXTON, WILLIAM (?). *Ars moriendi. The Craft for to Die for the Health of a
Man's Soul.* [1491; 1491; 1491]. That Caxton actually composed this text
is doubtful, and the identification of a source or sources is also doubtful
(see Wilson, pp. 796–97). University Microfilms, Reel 161, Bodleian
Library, Oxford.

———. Photolithographic copy by Edward W. B. Nicholson. London:
Bernard Quaritch; Oxford: Clarendon Press Depository [1891].

MIRK, JOHN. *The Festial.* 2nd ed. [1491; 1491; 1491].

MIRK, JOHN. *Four Sermons.* 3rd ed. (Duff lists as 2nd ed.) [1491; 1491; not
entered separately to *The Festial* in *New Cambridge Bibliography*].

BIRGITTA, SAINT (?). *Fifteen Oes,* tr. William Caxton. [1491; 1491; 1491].
Translated from a set of Latin prayers attributed to St. Birgitta. Contains
Caxton's Epilogue. University Microfilms, Reel 17, British Museum.

———. Photolithographic ed., Stephen Ayling. [London]: Griffith and
Farran, [1869].

Horae ad usum Sarum, 5th ed. [1491; not in Duff; not in *New Cambridge
Bibliography*]. Not seen.

Horae ad usum Sarum. 6th ed. [1491; not in Duff; not in *New Cambridge
Bibliography*]. Not seen. Consult Painter, pp. 184–86, on his identification of the fifth and sixth editions of the *Horae ad usum Sarum.*

See also:

JEROME, SAINT. *Vitas patrum,* tr. William Caxton. Westminster: Wynkyn de
Worde, 1495. Translated from a printed version, *Vie des peres* (Lyon,
1487), itself translated from the Latin *Vitas patrum* which is in part the
work of St. Jerome. Translated by Caxton in 1491 but not printed by
him. See Wilson, pp. 801–802. University Microfilms, Reel 2, British
Museum.

CAXTON, WILLIAM, tr. *The Metamorphoses of Ovid.* Not known to have
been printed by Caxton or by any other early printer. Caxton translated
from a French translation of Ovid. Contains Caxton's Colophon.

———. Books X–XV. Ed. S. Gaselee and H. F. B. Brett-Smith. Boston and
New York: Houghton Mifflin Company; Oxford: Basil Blackwell for the
Shakespeare Head Press, Stratford-upon-Avon, 1924.

———. Books I–XV. 2 vols. Facsimile. New York: George Braziller Inc.,
1968.

Caxton records preparing a *Life of Robert Earl of Oxford,* but no copy is
known.

For modern collections of materials from Caxton, see Secondary Sources, below, under Aurner, Blades, Blake, and Crotch.

SECONDARY SOURCES
(See Notes and References for additional material)

AURNER, NELLIE SLAYTON. *Caxton, Mirrour of Fifteenth-Century Letters: A Study of the Literature of the First English Press.* Boston and New York: Houghton Mifflin Company, 1926. Focuses on fifteenth century letters. Appendix: "Caxton's Prologues, Epilogues, and Interpolations."

BENNETT, H[ENRY] S[TANLEY]. *English Books & Readers, 1475 to 1557, Being a Study in the History of the Book Trade from Caxton to the Incorporation of the Stationers' Company.* Cambridge: University Press, 1952. Clearly presented and well authenticated.

BLADES, WILLIAM. *The Biography and Typography of William Caxton, England's First Printer.* 2nd rev. ed. London: Trübner & Co.; Strassburg: Karl I. Trübner, 1882. Reprinted, with an introduction by James Moran. London: Frederick Muller, 1971. Published in two volumes under the title *Life and Typography of William Caxton* in 1861–1863; condensed into one volume in 1877; reissued in the condensed form with revisions in 1882. Includes extensive selections from and facsimiles of Caxton's work. Though in need of correction in light of new discoveries, still a basic tool for Caxton studies.

BLAKE, N. F. *Caxton and his World.* Elmsford, New York, and London: House & Maxwell, British Book Centre, Inc., 1969. See below.

———. *Caxton: England's First Publisher.* London: Osprey, 1976. This and the entry above are companion volumes: the first on Caxton's literary contribution; the second on his work as a printer.

———, ed. *Caxton's Own Prose.* London: André Deutsch, 1973. Prologues, epilogues, and all else which can be identified as composed by Caxton except tables of contents and the like. Critical apparatus; glossary.

BÜHLER, CURT F. "The Binding of Books Printed by William Caxton," *Papers of the Bibliographical Society of America,* XXXVIII (1944), 1–8. Examination of what a book may reveal about its own making.

———. *The Fifteenth Century Book: The Scribes, The Printers, The Decorators.* Philadelphia: Pennsylvania University Press; London: Oxford University Press, 1960. Authoritative study.

———. *William Caxton and His Critics.* Syracuse, N.Y.: Syracuse University Press, 1960. Able defense of Caxton as a man and an editor.

BUTLER, PIERCE. *Legenda Aurea—Légende Dorée—Golden Legend.* Baltimore: J. Murphy Co., 1899. Old but basic source study.

BYLES, A. T. P. "William Caxton as a Man of Letters." *Library: Transactions of the Bibliographical Society,* 4th series, XV (1934), 1–25. Defends Caxton's judgment.

CARUS-WILSON, ELEANORA M. *Medieval Merchant Venturers: Collected Studies*. London: Methuen & Co., Ltd., 1954. Valuable study of the group to which Caxton belonged.

COLVILE, K. N. "William Caxton: Man of Letters," *Quarterly Review*, CCXLVIII (1927), 165–78.

CROTCH, W. J. B[LYTH], ed. *The Prologues and Epilogues of William Caxton*. Early English Text Society, Original Series, CLXXVI. London: Geoffrey Cumberlege, Oxford University Press, 1928; rpt. 1956. Subject to some correction but perhaps the single most useful book on Caxton. Contains biographical sketch, review of relevant documents, and reprints of Caxton's Prologues and Epilogues.

CUSAK, BRIDGET. "*Not wreton with penne and ynke:* Problems of Selection Facing the First English Printer." In *Edinburgh Studies in English and Scots*, ed. A. J. Aitken, Angus McIntosh, and Hermann Pálsson, pp. 29–54. London: Longman, 1971. Examines a significant problem.

DEACON, RICHARD. *A Biography of William Caxton, The First English Editor, Printer, Merchant, and Translator*. London: Frederick Muller, 1976. Speculative general study.

DE RICCI, SEYMOUR. *A Census of Caxtons*. Bibliographical Society, Illustrated Monographs, XV. London: Oxford University Press, 1909. Undertakes to locate and describe every known Caxton item. Indispensable though old.

DISRAELI, ISAAC. [*A Trilogy on Printing History*]. Cincinnati: Stratford Press, 1942. Dispraises the man and the printer.

DUFF, E. GORDON. *A Century of the English Book Trade: Short Notices of All Printers, Stationers, Book-Binders, and Others Connected with It from the Issue of the First Dated Book in 1457 to the Incorporation of the Company of Stationers in 1557*. London: Printed for the Bibliographical Society by Blades, East & Blades, 1905. List and brief identification of persons connected with the book trade.

———. *Fifteenth Century English Books: A Bibliography of Books and Documents Printed in England and of Books for the English Market Printed Abroad*. Bibliographical Society, Illustrated Monographs, XVIII. London: Oxford University Press, 1917; rpt. Meisenheim, Ger.: Hain, 1964. Essential for the study of English incunabula.

———. *William Caxton*. Chicago: Caxton Club, 1905. One hundred and forty-eight of the two hundred and fifty-two copies printed contain a single leaf from an imperfect copy of Caxton's first edition of *The Canterbury Tales*.

GOFF, FREDERICK R., comp. *Incunabula in American Libraries: A Third Census of Fifteenth-Century Books Recorded in North American Collections*. New York: Bibliographical Society of America, 1964; rpt. 1974. Essential.

GOLDSCHMIDT, E. PH. *Medieval Texts and their First Appearance in Print*. Supplement to the Bibliographical Society's Transactions XVI. London:

Bibliographical Society, 1943. Interesting speculation about Caxton and the Flores S. Augustini press at Cologne.

HALL, LOUIS BREWER. "Caxton's *Eneydos* and the Redactions of Vergil." *Mediaeval Studies*, XXII (1960), 136–47. Defends Caxton's much berated translation as a harbinger of the Renaissance.

HEILBRONNER, WALTER L. *Printing and the Book in Fifteenth-Century England: A Bibliographical Survey*. Charlottesville: Published for the Bibliographical Society of the University of Virginia, University Press of Virginia, 1967. Well-indexed annotated bibliography.

HIRSCH, RUDOLF. *Printing, Selling & Reading, 1450–1550*. Wiesbaden, Ger · Otto Harrassowitz, 1967. Solid review of the evidence on an elusive point; bears on Caxton's career.

JENNETT, SEAN. *Pioneers in Printing*. London: Routledge and Kegan Paul Ltd., 1958. Excellent introduction.

KEKEWICH, MARGARET. "Edward IV, William Caxton, and Literary Patronage in Yorkist England." *Modern Language Review*, LXVI (1971), 481–87. Title annotates.

KERLING, NELLY J. M. "Caxton and the Trade in Printed Books." *Book Collector*, IV (1955), 190–99. Studies a little known aspect of Caxton's work—as an importer of books.

KINGSFORD, CHARLES LETHBRIDGE. *English Historical Literature in the Fifteenth Century*. Oxford: Clarendon Press, 1913. Sets Caxton's historical volumes in context.

LATHROP, HENRY B. "The First English Printers and Their Patrons." *Library: Transactions of the Bibliographical Society*, 4th series, III (1922), 69–96. Argues for Caxton's dependence on patrons.

MCCARTHY, TERENCE. "Caxton and the Text of Malory's Book 2." *Modern Philology*, LXXI (1973), 144–52. Concerned with Caxton's role as editor and the unresolved problem of a definitive text of Malory.

MARKLAND, MURRAY F. "The Role of William Caxton." *Research Studies, Washington State University*, XXVIII (1960), 47–60. Speculates on the immediate impact of the printing press.

MONTGOMERY, ROBERT L. "William Caxton and the Beginning of Tudor Critical Thought." *Huntington Library Quarterly*, XXXVI (1973), 91–103. Sees Caxton as "a man of his age" (p. 103), more interested in books for what they teach than for their poetry.

MORAN, JAMES. "William Caxton and the Origins of English Publishing." *Gutenberg-Jahrbuch*, XLII (1967), 61–64. New consideration of an old problem.

MORGAN, PAUL. "A Caxton Discovery at Warwick." *The Times Literary Supplement*, LXIV (January 18, 1957), 40. Announces the discovery of a copy of the *Legenda secundum usum Sarum* previously known only from fragments.

MURPHY, JAMES J. "Caxton's Two Choices: 'Modern' and 'Medieval' Rhetoric in Traversagni's *Nova Rhetorica* and the Anonymous *Court of*

Sapience." Medievalia et Humanistica, new series, III (1972), 241–55.
Considers Caxton's contribution to English rhetoric.

[OLDYS, WILLIAM]. *Biographia Britannica.* London: W. Innys, etc., 1748.
II, 1223–49. Charming old account of Caxton.

PAINTER, GEORGE D. *William Caxton: A Quincentenary Biography of
England's First Printer.* London: Chatto & Windus, 1976. Painter's
"Foreword," p. vii, states that he has "described and discussed every
known Caxton document and edition . . . . [and] tried to rectify the
disconcertingly many established and hitherto unsuspected errors of
fact or inference in the work of . . . others." New proposal for the
chronology of Caxton's books.

PLOMER, H.R. "The Importation of Books into England in the Fifteenth and
Sixteenth Centuries: An Examination of Some Custom Rolls." *Library:
Transactions of the Bibliographical Society,* 4th series, IV (1923),
146–50. Casts some light on what was available to readers in Caxton's
day.

POLLARD, A[LFRED] W., and G. R. Redgrave. *A Short-Title Catalogue of
Books Printed in England, Scotland, & Ireland, and of English Books
Printed Abroad, 1475–1640.* London: Bibliographical Society, 1946.
With an *Index of Printers, Publishers, and Booksellers,* compiled by Paul
G. Morrison. Charlottesville: Bibliographical Society of the University
of Virginia; and London: Quaritch, 1950; second impression with
corrections, 1961. Of untold value to bibliographical studies.

ROBERTS, W. WRIGHT. "William Caxton, Writer and Critic." *Bulletin of the
John Rylands Library,* XIV (1930), 410–22. Valuable assessment of
Caxton as a literary figure.

SANDS, DONALD B. "Caxton as a Literary Critic." *Papers of the Bibliographical Society of America,* LI (1957), 312–18. Evaluates the probable
marketability of Caxton's books.

SCHLAUCH, MARGARET. *Antecedents of the English Novel: 1400–1600 (from
Chaucer to Deloney).* Warszawa: PWN-Polish Scientific Publishers;
London: Oxford University Press, 1963; rpt. 1965. Useful context for
Caxton's prose narratives.

THRUPP, SYLVIA L. *The Merchant Class of Medieval London, [1300–1500].*
Chicago: University of Chicago Press, 1948. Basic study of Caxton's
class.

UHLENDORF, B.A. "The Invention of Printing and Its Spread till 1470 with
Especial Reference to Social and Economic Factors." *Library Quarterly,* II (1931), 179–231. Careful analysis of the evidence concerning the
development of typography.

WATSON, GEORGE, ed. *The New Cambridge Bibliography of English
Literature,* I. Cambridge: University Press, 1974. See columns 667–74;
basic list of Caxton's books; secondary bibliography.

WELLS, JAMES. *William Caxton: A Paper Read Before The Caxton Club on
January 31, 1958.* Chicago: The Caxton Club, 1960. Takes Caxton's

great achievements to be his choice of books and his publishing chiefly in English.

WILSON, ROBERT H. "Malory and Caxton." In *A Manual of the Writings in Middle English 1050–1500*, gen. ed. Albert E. Hartung. New Haven: Connecticut Academy of Arts and Sciences, 1972. Vol. III, pp. 771–807, 924–51. Valuable primary and secondary bibliography.

WINSHIP, GEORGE PARKER. *William Caxton & His Work: A Paper Read at a Meeting of the Club of Odd Volumes . . in January 1908*. Berkeley: The Book Arts Club, University of California, 1937. Attempts to establish the real dimensions of Caxton's accomplishments.

————. *William Caxton and the First English Press: A Bio-Bibliographical Essay on the Life of the Governor of the English Nation in Burgundy, the Editor of the First Printed Work on English History, the First Publisher of the Canterbury Tales, and the First English Essayist: Together with an Original Leaf of the Polychronicon*. New York: Edmond Byrne Hackett, The Brick Row Book Shop, Inc., 1938. Winship has done extensive and valuable work on Caxton.

WORKMAN, SAMUEL K. *Fifteenth Century Translation as an Influence on English Prose*. Princeton Studies in English, No. 18. Princeton, N.J.: Princeton University Press, 1940. Studies the importance of translation as a literary art and of Caxton as a translator.

WORMALD, FRANCIS, and C. E. WRIGHT, eds. *The English Library before 1700: Studies in Its History*. [London]: University of London, Athlone Press, 1958. Essays on the state of English books before, during, and after Caxton's lifetime.

Index

Materials translated by Caxton are listed in the index under Caxton, William, Works Translated By. Materials published or probably intended for publication by him are entered under Caxton, William, Texts Published By or Translated for Probable Publication. The index locates publications and translations appearing in the text and in the bibliography of primary materials, where most of them are further described in the annotations. Caxton's prologues, epilogues, and other original writings as cited or quoted in the text are entered in the index under Caxton, William, Original Writing By; detailed indications of texts containing original writing by Caxton are given in the annotations to the primary bibliography. Texts translated and/or published by Caxton and cited in the text are also entered in index under their respective titles. Those with known authors or translators are cross referenced to author or translator (but not generally to both). Books commonly referred to in Caxton studies by various titles, including titles in more than one language, are generally entered under two or more titles. Scholars are identified in the notes and references and in the secondary bibliography; only in the few cases of some special use having been made of their work are scholars cited in the index.